THE AMSTERDAM CITY GUIDE

THE
AMSTERDAM
CITY GUIDE

YOUR LITTLE BLACK BOOK

TERRA

© 2016
Uitgeverij TERRA
Terra is part of TerraLannoo bv
P.O. Box 97
3990 DB Houten, The Netherlands
info@terralannoo.nl
www.terralannoo.nl

Author: Anne de Buck, YOURLITTLEBLACKBOOK.ME

Graphic design & layout: Daphne van Langen / RAZA, Amsterdam
Correction: Medea Sonneveld
Translation: Siji Jabbar, The English Writer, Amsterdam
Cartography: EMK, Deventer
Photography: Desiré van den Berg: 42; © Presstigieux: 8, 122; Beemflights: 98-99;
Jasper de Waal: 12, 33, 50-51, 74-75, 100, 107, 124-125, 126, 150, 172-173, 176, 180

First print, 2016

ISBN 978 90 8989 696 4
NUR 511

The information in this book is subject to change. Therefore, always check the website in question before visiting. The publisher is not liable for any consequences arising from the use of this book.

EAT WELL
TRAVEL
OFTEN

Cottoncake

CONTENTS

CONTENTS

IN LOVE WITH AMSTERDAM

I wake up in a different city almost every week, but Amsterdam remains my most beloved. *The Amsterdam City Guide*, with my favourite spots in the nicest neighbourhoods in the city, is the crown jewel of Your Little Black Book. For as long as I can remember, I have dreamt of living in Amsterdam at least once in my life. As a young girl from the provinces, the city held something magical. That was where everything happened! Cycling along the canals, the shops, a cosy café on every street corner – Amsterdam *has it all*. As a teenager, I visited Amsterdam whenever I could, to shop, club or attend festivals. And now that I've lived here for ten years, I can say with my hand on my heart: Amsterdam and I belong together.

My urban travel platform Your Little Black Book actually originated in this love affair with Amsterdam. Because what I love about cities is that there's always something new to discover. So every day I share the best spots in the city on Yourlittleblackbook.me, and offer tips every weekend on things to do in Amsterdam. In so doing my site has grown to become the largest urban travel blog in the Netherlands. As a professional travel blogger, I am now living my dream and travelling the world!

Cities are constantly changing: neighbourhoods that you previously wouldn't stoop to visit are now the trendiest parts of the city. Concept stores are where it's at when shopping for unique items. It's there that you find carefully curated collections of items that come with a story. The restaurant scene has evolved from traditional brown cafés and bistros to the most beautifully designed restaurants and bars. Whether you're after a five-course dinner or the day's special, your taste buds will be satisfied with help from this *City Guide*.

I love the diversity of Amsterdam, my big tiny city. Everything is here, and yet when you stroll through the neighbourhoods described in this book you feel as though you're in a small town. From the rugged Amsterdam North to the up-and-coming Baarsjes, the beautiful canal district and the cosy Jordaan. I offer tips to check off your Amsterdam bucket list in every neighbourhood, and a tour of my personal favourite hotspots. To make your life even easier, I also provide shortlists, from the nicest coffee bars to where to go for breakfast or to shop.

Enjoy!
Love,
Anne de Buck

YOURLITTLEBLACKBOOK.ME | ANNE@YOURLITTLEBLACKBOOK.ME | @YOURLBB (ALL SOCIAL-MEDIA CHANNELS)

Central Station

Busy planning a trip to Amsterdam? Discover how to avoid looking like a tourist on your rented bicycle. Buy tickets for that awesome festival happening while you're in town, and find out when you need to go casual or dress up to leave your hotel room or apartment. Discover Amsterdam like a proper local with these practical tips!

365 DAYS

You can have the perfect city trip anytime of the year. Each season possesses its own charm and cool events not to miss while you're in town!

SPRING

At the first hint of sunshine, everyone flocks to the city's terraces. The food-festival season starts again and the city turns orange on King's Day.

Must-see events:
- King's Day – 27 APRIL
- Amsterdam Coffee Festival
  AMSTERDAMCOFFEEFESTIVAL.COM – MARCH
- Liberation Day – 5 MAY
- De Rollende Keukens
  (food truck festival)
  ROLLENDEKEUKENS.AMSTERDAM – MAY
- Taste of Amsterdam
  TASTEOFAMSTERDAM.COM – JUNE
- World Press Photo
  WORLDPRESSPHOTO.ORG – APRIL/JULY
- Opening of festival season – FROM APRIL

SUMMER

Amsterdam is awesome in the summer. Every week there's a festival where you can dance the whole day through. Boats sail along the canals and the parks are packed with picnic rugs.

Must-see events:
- Amsterdam Fashionweek
  FASHIONWEEK.NL – JULY
- Dance festivals
- Vondelpark open-air concerts
  OPENLUCHTTHEATER.NL – JULY & AUGUST
- Gay Pride
  AMSTERDAMGAYPRIDE.NL – AUGUST
- Grachtenfestival (Canal festival)
  GRACHTENFESTIVAL.NL – AUGUST
- Artis ZOOmeravonden
  (Artis Zoo summer evenings)
  ARTIS.NL – JUNE/AUGUST
- Sail SAIL.NL – ONCE EVERY FIVE YEARS

AUTUMN

The season when nightlife once again moves back to the clubs, new restaurants throw open their doors and we descend on the pubs en masse with friends.

Must-see events:
- Amsterdam Dance Event
  AMSTERDAM-DANCE-EVENT.NL – OCTOBER
- Jordaan Festival
  JORDAANFESTIVAL.NL – SEPTEMBER
- Heritage Day
  OPENMONUMENTENDAG.NL – SEPTEMBER
- Museum Night MUSEUMNACHT.AMSTERDAM
  – NOVEMBER
- Amsterdam Marathon, TCSAMSTERDAM-
  MARATHON.NL – OKTOBER
- IDFA IDFA.NL – NOVEMBER

GOOD TO KNOW

WINTER

Ice-skating at the Museumplein.
Red wine and cheese plates in
cafés. And Christmas markets for
hours of wandering.

Must-see events:

- Amsterdam Light Festival
  AMSTERDAMLIGHTFESTIVAL.COM
  DECEMBER – JANUARY
- Christmas – 25 & 26 DECEMBER
- New Year's Eve – 31 DECEMBER
- Amsterdam Fashionweek
  FASHIONWEEK.NL – JANUARY

TIP!
Amsterdam
looks even more
magnificent from
the canals, so
hire a boat.

Nothing beats exploring the city
like a local. Of course you'll want
to see the tourist highlights the
first time you visit the city. But
it's immersion in the local culture
and contact with locals that often
provide those special moments
you reminisce about years later.

- Rent a bike via THEHUMBLEVINTAGE.NL
and you won't look like the typical
tourist on a standard rented bike.
You can rent Dutch bikes or
hipster racing bikes here.
- Stay at an Airbnb apartment in
a residential area outside the city
centre and discover Amsterdam
through your host's eyes.
- Join an Amsterdammer for
dinner at home via EATWITH.COM.
- Book a tour via TRIP4REAL.COM
and discover the city through a
local – from bike tours to cooking
classes.
- Rent yourself a boat via sites like
BOOTJEHURENINAMSTERDAM.COM, fill
a picnic basket with goodies and
cruise the canals!

GETTING AROUND

Amsterdam is very accessible by public transport. You can travel quite easily by train from Schiphol airport straight to Central Station in the heart of the city.

• Coming by car? Be aware that parking along the canals can cost up to €5 per hour. So park at a reduced rate in one of the parking garages, or for even less at a P + R (Park + Ride) outside the city centre. AMSTERDAM.NL/PARKEREN-VERKEER

• Uber taxi service operates in Amsterdam. You can order a taxi quite easily via the app, wherever you are. Prefer a regular taxi? Call 020-7777777 and order one from TCA.

• The bicycle is the vehicle of choice in Amsterdam. Still rather travel by tram, bus or tube? You can plan your journey with ease via 9292.NL. You'll need an ov-chipcard for public transport. Buy one from a ticket machine at any station and load it up with credit. You can also pay for your ticket in cash on trams, but that'll cost you a bit more. GVB.NL, OV-CHIPKAART.NL

• Amsterdam looks even more beautiful from the water. Go to Amsterdam North by ferry, which will take you across the IJ river for free from behind Central Station. Very touristy but no less fun are the tour boats (which is something every local ought to try at least once!) Or take a hop-on hop-off Canal Bus. CANAL.NL

EATING HABITS

Amsterdam is one of the most easy-going cities in Europe. Generally speaking, Amsterdammers are relaxed, straight-forward and down-to-earth. A few things worth knowing:

• Getting from A to B is quickest by bike, rented or otherwise.

• Eating out is a social activity here, so take the time to make the most of it.

• Restaurants are usually already full by 7pm during the week; weekend reservations are typically made for between 8 and 9pm.

• Amsterdammers only dress up for really fancy restaurants, so you're quite safe leaving your smart jacket and high heels at home.

• Saturday and Sunday brunch is becoming increasingly popular in Amsterdam.

• Barbecuing in the park is only permitted in designated areas.

• Amsterdam has quite a lively house scene, which you see reflected in the clubs and at festivals.

• Most shops and museums also open on Sundays.

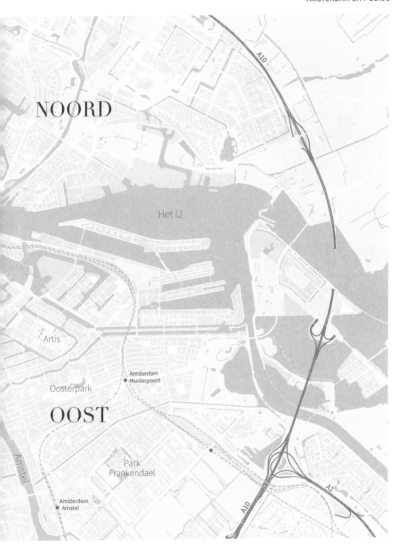

NOORD

Het IJ

AMSTERDAM

Artis

Oosterpark

OOST

Amsterdam
Muiderpoort

Park
Frankendael

Amstel

Amsterdam
Amstel

A10

A10

A1

BUCKET LIST

Rollende Keukens

A bucket list of things every Amsterdammer and visitor ought to do in Amsterdam at least once in their lives: Popular and less well-known must-dos, from the classic and refined to the wild and new. Tick them off your bucket list one at a time. Too many to fit in a weekend, so you'll always have a reason to return to Amsterdam.

- ☐ Cycling along the canals
- ☐ Barbecuing in the Vondelpark
- ☐ NDSM Wharf
- ☐ Museum of Bags & Purses
- ☐ Street Art Tour
- ☐ Cheese-tasting at Kef
- ☐ Gerard Doustraat
- ☐ Brandt en Levie sausage workshop
- ☐ The Foodhallen
- ☐ Concert at the Concertgebouw
- ☐ Dim sum at Oriental City
- ☐ Festival at Ruigoord
- ☐ Haarlemmerstraat & Haarlemmerdijk
- ☐ Clubbing at De School
- ☐ Van Gogh Museum
- ☐ De Negen Straatjes (The Nine Streets)
- ☐ Koningsdag (King's Day)
- ☐ Museum Night
- ☐ IJ-hallen
- ☐ Eating raw haring
- ☐ Foam

- ☐ Lookout at A'DAM Toren (Tower)
- ☐ Visit a café in Amsterdam's Jordaan
- ☐ Amsterdam Museum
- ☐ Tuschinski
- ☐ Ferry to North
- ☐ Rijksmuseum
- ☐ Food trucks in the Vondelpark
- ☐ Dinner at the Vuurtoreneiland
- ☐ Sail along the canals
- ☐ Eat bitterballs
- ☐ Stedelijk Museum
- ☐ Syrup cookies at the Albert Cuyp market
- ☐ Eat dinner at Rijsel
- ☐ Sunday markets
- ☐ Anne Frank House
- ☐ See Amsterdam from a rooftop
- ☐ De Rollende Keukens (food truck festival)
- ☐ Watch the sunset at Pllek
- ☐ Tropenmuseum (Museum of the Tropics)
- ☐ Beer-tasting at a craft brewery
- ☐ Cycle through the Rijksmuseum tunnel

BUCKET LIST

Rijsel

SHORT LISTS

Lists with summaries of the best tips – this is something we love at Your Little Black Book. In these themed shortlists you'll find all our favourites in a row. Because sometimes you're simply not in the mood to search or read. From the best hotels to coffee bars, and from concept stores to nightlife.

15 X FINEST HOTELS

That you'll only ever visit your hotel to sleep is no reason to pick an old-fashioned one. A nice hotel with both a decent bed *and* a beautiful interior can make a city trip even more enjoyable. You may want something very luxurious or romantic, something sleek, or something designerish on a budget. We've therefore created this shortlist of Amsterdam's nicest hotels.

❶ The Hoxton

You don't go to The Hoxton just to sleep. The lobby is popular with trendy locals meeting for coffee or cocktails. The rooms are slickly designed, and with a bit of luck you'll get one overlooking the canals. Hang your breakfast bag on your outer doorknob and your breakfast will be ready by the door by the time you wake up. Cool events are organised weekly at The Hoxton.

HERENGRACHT 255, THEHOXTON.COM

❷ Hotel De Hallen

Hotel De Hallen is located in a former tram depot in Amsterdam Old-West. Rooms at this designer hotel have beautiful interiors and are very luxurious. Many of the building's original details remain visible. You'll find a cinema in the building next door, as well as indoor food market The Foodhallen, which

you definitely should not miss. Breakfast is served at Remise47, where you can also get a tasty meal in the evening.

BELLAMYPLEIN 47, HOTELDEHALLEN.COM

❸ Conservatorium hotel

You'll find the Conservatorium hotel in a beautiful building next to the Museumplein, along with restaurant Taiko, one of the best Japanese restaurants in town. As the name suggests, the building once housed a conservatory. You will want for nothing if you stay here. Make sure you order room service for breakfast so you can enjoy your room a little longer. Then go relax in the luxurious Akasha Spa for a perfect start to the day.

VAN BAERLESTRAAT 27, CONSERVATORIUMHOTEL.COM

4 Hotel Not Hotel

Every room is unique at Hotel Not Hotel. Designed by different artists, each room has a special story. You can sleep in an antique tram carriage, for example, or in one of the other affordable rooms. The lobby of this unique hotel is a large exhibition space with a homely atmosphere. Breakfast is served at Kevin Bacon, the bar and restaurant where you can eat and drink anytime of the day.

PIRI REISPLEIN 34,
HOTELNOTHOTEL.COM

5 Hotel V Nesplein

Always handy when you stay at a hotel that also serves tasty food. At Hotel V on the Nesplein you get a stylish room right in the heart of the city, one with industrial elements and decorated in warm colours. The Lobby restaurant is a must for lunch or dinner, and offers good value for money.

NES 49, HOTELVNESPLEIN.NL

6 Student Hotel

Affordable lodgings in Amsterdam East are to be had at the Student Hotel. The rooms are simple, but the lobby and common areas are furnished with the coolest

designer furniture. Students can stay for longer periods, but you can also book per night for a very reasonable price.

WIBAUTSTRAAT 129,
THESTUDENTHOTEL.COM

7 W Hotel

Whoever loves luxury and glamour will have a blast at W Hotel. Right in the city centre around the corner from Dam Square, what was once an old telecom building has been beautifully renovated and transformed into a luxury hotel. Restaurant Mr. Porter is open from breakfast time to the cocktail hour, and has a rooftop terrace with a mini swimming pool and a view of the palace on the Dam.

SPUISTRAAT 175, WAMSTERDAM.COM

8 Volkshotel

If you're staying at the Volkshotel, chances are that you'll be spending a lot of time at the hotel. It's an innovative concept with an urban design, and is named after the newspaper *de Volkskrant*, which for years had its editorial department in the building. It now has one of the nicest rooftop terraces in Amsterdam, restaurant Canvas – where you

can club after dinner – and cocktail bar Doka, which opens at weekends until 7 o'clock in the morning.
WIBAUTSTRAAT 150, VOLKSHOTEL.NL

9 Andaz Amsterdam

Whoever stays at the Andaz hotel will feel like one of the locals "living" in the city's Canal District. Located around the corner from the Nine Streets, you'll want for nothing at this beautiful five-star hotel on the Prinsengracht. This hotel was designed and furnished by internationally known Dutch designer Marcel Wanders. The restaurant Blue Spoon serves dishes made with local ingredients. Relax in the city spa after a day strolling the city!
PRINSENGRACHT 587, AMSTERDAM. PRINSENGRACHT.ANDAZ.HYATT.COM

10 Generator Hostel

If you travel a lot you'll probably have heard of Generator Hostels. This trendy hostel is located right next to the Oosterpark in booming Amsterdam East. Don't be fooled by the word "hostel", because in addition to dormitories you can also book private rooms. The building was once the home of the

University of Amsterdam's Faculty of Health Sciences. The restaurant and speakeasy bar in the basement are open to both guests and locals.
MAURITSKADE 57, GENERATORHOSTELS.COM

11 City Hub

The best of hotels and hostels are brought together at City Hub: the sociability of a hostel (with a coolly furnished common room), but with your own private "hub" for sleeping. Each hub is equipped with the latest technological gadgets and a huge double bed. Affordable lodgings for whoever prefers to spend their money on good food and drink. And that you can do only too well in the neighbourhood of City Hub!
BELLAMYSTRAAT 3, CITYHUB.COM

12 Sir Adam

Amsterdam North is the most rugged part of the city and Sir Adam is where to stay. This urban luxury boutique is located in A'DAM: the creative hub in the massive square tower across the IJ from Central Station. The hotel occupies the tower's lower eight floors, and includes The Butcher Social Club restaurant,

a terrace overlooking the IJ, and a beer garden.
OVERHOEKSPLEIN 1, ADAMTOREN.NL

13 Morgan & Mees

Locals know Morgan & Mees especially for its good restaurant and cosy bar. A priceless tip for anyone who'd love to explore the Jordaan on foot from their hotel: you can also stay at Morgan & Mees. Its nine rooms are all individually decorated and so stylish that you'll barely be able to bring yourself to leave.
TWEEDE HUGO DE GROOTSTRAAT 2, MORGANANDMEES.COM

14 INK Hotel

This hotel in the city centre owes its name to the rich history of the building. This was originally the home of the newspaper *De Tijd*, but now you'll be staying in a fine lifestyle hotel. The rooms are atmospheric, with wood and crisp white linen bedding. In the Pressroom restaurant you can eat local dishes with a twist at any time of the day, or have a nice drinking session.
NIEUWEZIJDS VOORBURGWAL 67, MGALLERY.COM

15 Hotel Dwars

Hotel Dwars is located around the corner from the cosy Utrechtsestraat. The nine rooms were creatively decorated by concept store Things I Like, Things I Love. Each room is unique, with interiors a mix of new and vintage furniture. Original brick walls, warm colours, plants, and a beautiful quilt on every bed. A wonderful base from which to reach all the neighbourhood hotspots.
UTRECHTSEDWARSSTRAAT 79, HOTELDWARS.COM

28 X BEST RESTAURANTS

Everyone knows those restaurants you keep going back to again and again because the food, atmosphere and service are always great, and from which you always return home with a satisfied feeling after a night of wining and dining.

Fa. Speijkervet
The best restaurant in De Baarsjes, with a solid menu.
ADMIRAAL DE RUIJTERWEG 79, SPEIJKERVET.NL

Choux
Fantastic food, ditto the service; the cooking here is divine.
DE RUYTERKADE 128, CHOUX.NL

Sinne
Very good and affordable dining at this Michelin-starred restaurant in De Pijp.
CEINTUURBAAN 342, RESTAURANTSINNE.NL

Mos
Very good and extensive dining, with an awesome view over the IJ and Amsterdam North.
IJDOK 185, MOSAMSTERDAM.NL

Americano Bar & Kitchen
New York style Italian food in a classic interior in a gorgeous building on the Amstel.
AMSTELDIJK 25, BARAMERICANO.NL

Kaagman & Kortekaas
High-quality dining in a cosy bistro setting at this hidden gem in the heart of the city.
SINT NICOLAASSTRAAT 43, KAAGMANENKORTEKAAS.NL

De Luwte
De Luwte is tucked away in the Leliegracht, and is one restaurant you'll keep returning to.
LELIEGRACHT 26, RESTAURANTDELUWTE.NL

Hotel De Goudfazant
Once a car garage in North, now an industrial restaurant offering good value for money.
AAMBEELDSTRAAT 10H, HOTELDEGOUDFAZANT.NL

Wilde Zwijnen & Eetbar Wilde Zwijnen
A favourite for years; good seasonal food and always cosy.
JAVAPLEIN 23 & 25, WILDEZWIJNEN.COM

Rijsel
Housed in a former domestic science school in East, it serves finely crafted dishes with a French twist.
MARCUSSTRAAT 52, RIJSEL.COM

Daalder
A pub serving delicious dishes in the cosy Jordaan.
LINDENGRACHT 90, DAALDERAMSTERDAM.NL

Panache
The sort of restaurant where you linger over cocktails long after dinner.
TEN KATESTRAAT 117, CAFEPANACHE.NL

Restaurant C
Divine cooking from -20 tot 200 degrees Celsius.
WIBAUTSTRAAT 125, C.AMSTERDAM

Worst Wijncafé
Sausages take on a whole new meaning at this hidden gem.
BARENTSZSTRAAT 171, DEWORST.NL

Gebroeders Hartering
Great dishes with everything from head to tail; you will rhapsodize for days.
PEPERSTRAAT 10, GEBR-HARTERING.NL

Ron Gastrobar Oriental
Peking duck, superb dumplings and other high-level Asian culinary delights.
KERKSTRAAT 23, RONGASTROBARORIENTAL.NL

Morgan & Mees
Hotel restaurants are hot in Amsterdam, and this is one of the jewels in West.
TWEEDE HUGO DE GROOTSTRAAT 2, MORGANANDMEES.COM

Café De Klepel
One of the best gastropubs in Amsterdam, with a changing three-course menu.
PRINSENSTRAAT 22, CAFEDEKLEPEL.NL

Café Modern
An old bank converted into a table d'hôte restaurant with a seasonal menu.
MEIDOORNWEG 2, JACQUESJOUR.NL

Restaurant Breda
A neo bistro with fantastic food and wines.
SINGEL 210, BREDA-AMSTERDAM.COM

Salmuera
Good Argentinian steak, ceviche and cocktails, right in the city centre.
ROZENGRACHT 106, SAL-AMSTERDAM.NL

De Plantage
Gorgeous restaurant overlooking Artis Zoo, with an international menu.
PLANTAGE KERKLAAN 36, CAFERESTAUANTDEPLANTAGE.NL

Fa. Pekelhaaring

Vintage decor, affordable Italian cuisine and years of consistent quality.

VAN WOUSTRAAT 127–129, PEKELHAARING.NL

Balthazar's Keuken

One of the first table d'hôte restaurants in Amsterdam, and always lively fun.

ELANDSGRACHT 108, BALTHAZARSKEUKEN.NL

Guts & Glory

A different beast takes centre stage on the menu every season.

UTRECHTSESTRAAT 6, GUTSGLORY.NL

Toscanini

One of the city's best Italian restaurants, where time appears to stand still.

LINDENGRACHT 75, RESTAURANTTOSCANINI.NL

Gin Neo Bistro & Wines

A culinary evening in the Jordaan with good wines and food with a story.

WESTERSTRAAT 264, GINAMSTERDAM.COM

Restaurant DS

Wining and dining at the restaurant of club De School.

JAN VAN BREEMENSTRAAT 1, DESCHOOLAMSTERDAM.NL

SHORTLISTS

Kaagman & Kortekaas

22 X BREAKFAST, LUNCH & BRUNCH

The nicest spots for a scrumptious breakfast early in the morning, or a boozy brunch or lunch, serving the most delicious sandwiches and fresh juices.

Little Collins
Eerste Sweelinckstraat 19F
LITTLECOLLINS.NL – *breakfast: weekend*

Omelegg
Ferdinand Bolstraat 143
OMELEGG.COM

Bakers & Roasters
Eerste Jacob van Campenstraat 54
Kadijksplein 16
BAKERSANDROASTERS.COM

Scandinavian Embassy
Sarphatipark 34
SCANDINAVIANEMBASSY.NL

De Wasserette
Eerste van der Helststraat 27
DEWASSERETTE.COM

G's
Goudsbloemstraat 91
Linnaeusstraat 88
REALLYNICEPLACE.COM – *no breakfast*

CT coffee & coconuts
Ceintuurbaan 282
CTAMSTERDAM.NL

Boterham
Andreas Bonnstraat 2
BOTERHAM.AMSTERDAM – *no brunch*

Beter & Leuk
Eerste Oosterparkstraat 91
BETERENLEUK.NL

Cottoncake
Eerst van der Helststraat 76-HS
COTTONCAKE.NL

Staring at Jacob
Jacob van Lennepkade 215
STARINGATJACOB.NL – *only brunch*

Vinnies
Haarlemmerstraat 46
Nieuwezijds Kolk 33
VINNIESHOMEPAGE.COM

Pluk

Berry
Bilderdijkkade 27
BERRYAMSTERDAM.NL – *no brunch*

The Breakfast Club
Bellamystraat 2, Haarlemmerplein 31
THEBREAKFASTCLUB.NL

Bar Basquiat
Javastraat 88-90
BARBASQUIAT.NL

TEDS
Bosboom Toussaintstraat 60
TEDS-PLACE.NL

Lavinia Good Food
Kerkstraat 176
LAVINIAGOODFOOD.NL

Pluk
Reestraat 19
PLUK9STRAATJES.NL

Ninour
Eerste Jan Steenstraat 109
NINOUR.NL

Yay
Gerard Doustraat 74
YAYAMSTERDAM.NL – *no brunch*

Stek
Wibautstraat 95-97
STEK-AMSTERDAM.COM

De laatste kruimel
Langebrugsteeg 4
DELAATSTEKRUIMEL.NL – *no brunch*

11 X NICEST MARKETS

Nothing beats a weekend stroll among locals through an outdoor market. From foodie proof to vintage to typically Dutch, these are the markets you need to know in Amsterdam.

WEEKEND

Sunday Market
Once a month, the Westergas terrain turns into a shopping mecca for fashion, art and design by local artists and designers.
SUNDAYMARKET.NL – MONTHLY

NeighbourFood Market
Artisanal and tasty food made with local products alternates with second-hand curiosa at the Westergas terrain.
NEIGHBOURFOODMARKET.NL – MONTHLY

Local Goods Market
You can shop almost every week at the magnificent De Hallen complex in West for products either made or designed in Amsterdam.
FACEBOOK.COM/LOCALGOODSWEEKENDMARKET – FORTNIGHTLY

Amsterdam Blend Market
A platform for locals with stalls for vintage, design, local delicacies and music at varying locations.
AMSTERDAMBLENDMARKET.NL – MOSTLY MONTHLY

ORGANIC

Pure Markt
You'll find pure comestibles sold by the producers themselves at the Pure Market.
PUREMARKT.NL – EVERY MONTH

Farmers Market
Buy the tastiest organic produce straight from the farm at the Farmers Market.
• NOORDERMARKT, NOORDERMARKT-AMSTERDAM.NL
• NIEUWMARKT, FACEBOOK.COM/BIOLOGISCHE NIEUWMARKT – BOTH EVERY SATURDAY

TYPICALLY DUTCH

Albert Cuyp Market
Albert Cuyp, the most famous market in Amsterdam, is always pleasantly crowded and you can buy anything and everything here.
ALBERTCUYP.NL – EVERY DAY, EXCEPT SUNDAY

Pekmarkt
Van der Pekstraat in North is hot and the market Amsterdam-cosy. With an organic

TIP!
Go for a weekend brunch at a
food market.

market on Fridays and vintage at the
mixed market on Saturdays.
PEKMARKT.NL – WEDNESDAY, FRIDAY & SATURDAY

VINTAGE

Noordermarkt flea market
Between 9am and 1pm, this is *the*
destination for affordable vintage.
Go early for the best items!
JORDAANMARKTEN.NL – EVERY MONDAY

IJ-hallen
Huge flea market with hundreds of stalls
in an old warehouse on NDSM Wharf in
Amsterdam North.
IJ-HALLEN.NL – EVERY MONTH

Waterlooplein
This flea market has long been an
institution in Amsterdam and the place
to score original vintage.
WATERLOOPLEINMARKT.NL,
EVERY DAY, EXCEPT SUNDAY

8 X VINTAGE SHOPS

Amsterdam has lots of lovely
vintage shops where you can find
the most unique gems to suit any
budget.

1 Episode
NIEUWE SPIEGELSTRAAT 61 & BERENSTRAAT 1
& WATERLOOPLEIN 1 & SPUISTRAAT 96 &
PRINSENGRACHT 570, EPISODE.EU

2 Laura Dols
WOLVENSTRAAT 7, LAURADOLS.NL

3 Kilo Shop
JODENBREESTRAAT 158, FACEBOOK.COM/
KILOSHOPAMSTERDAM

4 We Are Vintage
KINKERSTRAAT 193 & EERSTE VAN SWINDEN-
STRAAT 43, WEAREVINTAGE.NL

5 Jutka en Riska
HAARLEMMERDIJK 143
& BILDERDIJKSTRAAT 194, JUTKAENRISKA.NL

6 Het Kaufhaus
EERSTE SWEELINCKSTRAAT 21,
HAARLEMMERDIJK 152-154, HETKAUFHAUS.NL

7 Marbles Vintage
HAARLEMMERDIJK 64 & FERDINAND
BOLSTRAAT 28 & STAALSTRAAT 30

8 Zipper
HUIDENSTRAAT 7 & NIEUWE HOOGSTRAAT 8,
ZIPPERSTORE.NL

SHORTLISTS

16 X DELICIOUS COFFEE

Of course you can get a coffee on pretty much any street corner in Amsterdam. But there's coffee and there's COFFEE. At these specialty coffee bars you can enjoy the very best coffee made from unique blends of coffee beans from around the world.

Bakers & Roasters
EERSTE JACOB VAN CAMPENSTRAAT 54 & KADIJKSPLEIN 16, BAKERSANDROASTERS.COM

Scandinavian Embassy
SARPHATIPARK 34, SCANDINAVIANEMBASSY.NL

CT coffee & coconuts
CEINTUURBAAN 282, CTAMSTERDAM.NL

Coffee Bru
BEUKENPLEIN 14, COFFEEBRU.NL

Bedford Stuyvesant
JAVASTRAAT 55, BEDFORDSTUYVESANT.NL

Rum Baba
PRETORIUSSTRAAT 33, FACEBOOK.COM/RUMBABABAKES

The Coffee Virus
OVERHOEKSPLEIN 2, THECOFFEEVIRUS.NL

Caffènation
WARMONDSTRAAT 120, FACEBOOK.COM/CAFFENATIONAMSTERDAM

Cut Throat Barber & Coffee
BEURSPLEIN 5, CUTTHROATBARBER.NL

Espresso Fabriek
PAZZANISTRAAT 39 & IJBURGLAAN 1489, ESPRESSOFABRIEK.NL

White Label Coffee
JAN EVERTSENSTRAAT 136, WHITELABELCOFFEE.NL

Bocca
KERKSTRAAT 96-98, BOCCA.NL

Toki
BINNEN DOMMERSSTRAAT 15, TOKIHO.AMSTERDAM

Filter
VALKENBURGERSTRAAT 124, FILTERAMSTERDAM.NL

Lot Sixty One
KINKERSTRAAT 112, LOTSIXTYONECOFFEE.COM

Two For Joy
HAARLEMMERDIJK 182, TWOFORJOY.NL

Bocca

Gathershop

16 X UNIQUE CONCEPT STORES

Each as different as the next, selling carefully curated items so beautiful and inspiring that you'll want to take everything home with you.

Cottoncake
EERSTE VAN DER HELSTSTRAAT 76, COTTONCAKE.NL

Anna + Nina
GERARD DOUSTRAAT 94 & KLOVENIERSBURGWAL 44, ANNA-NINA.NL

Things I Like, Things I Love
CEINTUURBAAN 69 & JAN EVERTSENSTRAAT 106, THINGSILIKETHINGSILOVE.COM

Hutspot
VAN WOUSTRAAT 4 & ROZENGRACHT 204-210, HUTSPOTAMSTERDAM.COM

All the Luck in the World
GERARD DOUSTRAAT 86 & LINNAEUSSTRAAT 20, ALLTHELUCKINTHEWORLD.NL

Tenue de Nîmes
HAARLEMMERSTRAAT 92-94 & ELANDSGRACHT 60, TENUEDENIMES.COM

Gathershop
VAN WOUSTRAAT 99, GATHERSHOP.NL

Hartje Oost
JAVASTRAAT 23, HARTJEOOST.NL

Draagbaar
SUMATRASTRAAT 54, DRAAGBAAR.NU

T.I.T.S.
DE CLERCQSTRAAT 78, TITS-STORE.COM

Friday Next
OVERTOOM 31, FRIDAYNEXT.COM

MaisonNL
UTRECHTSESTRAAT 118, MAISONNL.COM

Robins Hood
TWEEDE TUINDWARSSTRAAT 7, ROBINSHOOD.NL

Restored
HAARLEMMERDIJK 39, RESTORED.NL

Six and Sons
HAARLEMMERDIJK 31, SIXANDSONS.COM

Concrete Matter
HAARLEMMERDIJK 127, CONCRETE-MATTER.COM

12 X RED LIGHT DISTRICT

The Red Light District has so much more to offer than strip clubs, peep shows and dodgy bars. Be amazed by the foodie spots on this shortlist and you will forever think differently of Amsterdam's Red Light District!

RESTAURANTS

Restaurant Anna
High-class dining at the foot of the Oude Kerk.
WARMOESSTRAAT 111, RESTAURANTANNA.NL

ArtDeli
Exquisite dining surrounded by extraordinary works of art in a monumental listed building.
ROKIN 93, ART-DELI.COM

Mata Hari
A typical all-day hotspot where it's cosy from morning till evening.
OUDEZIJDS ACHTERBURGWAL 22,
MATAHARI-AMSTERDAM.NL

Blauw aan de Wal
Via an alley you emerge into a courtyard where this atmospheric restaurant is located.
OUDEZIJDS ACHTERBURGWAL 99,
BLAUWAANDEWAL.COM

COFFEE & LUNCH

Quartier Putain
For good coffee and live music.
OUDEKERKSPLEIN 4A, QUARTIERPUTAIN.NL

Cut Throat Barber & Coffee
Coffee, lunch and a professional shave by the barber.
BEURSPLEIN 5, CUTTHROATBARBER.NL

Omelegg
All-day brunch with various egg dishes.
NIEUWEBURGSTEEG 24, OMELEGG.COM

Ivy & Bros
For coffee and a nice selection of cookware.
OUDEZIJDS VOORBURGWAL 96A,
FACEBOOK.COM/IVYANDBROS

LITE/DARK
Health food and lip-smacking juices in a bright interior.
ZEEDIJK 59, LITEDARK.NL

TIP!
You often find the most
extraordinary exhibitions at the Oude Kerk
in the Red Light District

Koko Coffee & Design
You come here not only for the good coffee, but also for the beautiful fashion and lifestyle brands on offer.
OUDEZIJDS ACHTERBURGWAL 145,
ILOVEKOKO.COM

DRINKS

Porem
For the best cocktails in the Red Light District.
GELDERSEKADE 17, POREMAMSTERDAM.COM

Brouwerij de Prael
For craft beers brewed on site.
OUDEZIJDS VOORBURGWAL 30, DEPRAEL.NL

6 X CHINATOWN
Don't expect designer interiors and trendy dishes. Yet at these basic spots in the Red Light District you can enjoy the tastiest Asian food!

1 **Hoi Tin** – Dim Sum
ZEEDIJK 122-124, RESTAURANTHOITIN.COM

2 **Snackbar Bird** – Thais
ZEEDIJK 72-74, THAI-BIRD.NL

3 **Nam Kee** – Chinees
ZEEDIJK 111-113, NAMKEE.NET

4 **Little Saigon** – Vietnamees
ZEEDIJK 88-90, LITTLESAIGON.NL

5 **New King** – Chinees
ZEEDIJK 115-117, NEWKING.NL

6 **Yokiyo** – Korean BBQ
OUDEZIJDS VOORBURGWAL 67, YOKIYO.NL

SHORTLISTS

9 X SUMMER IN THE CITY

Amsterdammers fill the terraces as soon as the first sunrays hit the city. This is a wonderful city in summertime, with city beaches next to the water, rooftop terraces and summer hotspots in the city centre. These are tips for keeping yourself entertained once the mercury rises above 20 degrees.

ROOFTOP TERRACES

Canvas
WIBAUTSTRAAT 150, VOLKSHOTEL.NL

Mr. Porter
SPUISTRAAT 175, MRPORTERSTEAKHOUSE.COM

Floor 17
STAALMEESTERSLAAN 410, FLOOR17.NL

URBAN BEACHES

Amsterdam Roest
JACOB BONTIUSPLAATS 1, AMSTERDAMROEST.NL

Pllek
TT NEVERITAWEG 59, PLLEK.NL

Blijburg
PAMPUSLAAN 501, BLIJBURG.NL

SUMMER HOTSPOTS

Hannekes Boom
DIJKSGRACHT 4, HANNEKESBOOM.NL

Café De Ceuvel
KORTE PAPAVERWEG 2, CAFEDECEUVEL.NL

Waterkant
MARNIXSTRAAT 246, WATERKANTAMSTERDAM.NL

PSSSST...

Okay, fast-forward for a couple of winter tips! When it's cold outside, it's wonderful to curl up in front of the fireplace at one of these hotspots.

FIREPLACES

The Lobby
NES 49, THELOBBY-AMSTERDAM.NL

The Vergulden Eenhoorn
RINGDIJK 58, VERGULDENEENHOORN.NL

The Duchess
SPUISTRAAT 172, THE-DUCHESS.COM

SHORTLISTS

Hannekes Boom

Porem

16 X NIGHTLIFE

Amsterdam is the capital of dance music. Old warehouses, schools and office buildings have been converted into nightclubs playing techno, deep house and electro. Some of them even have 24-hour licenses, so the party carries on as long as there are clubbers present. Prefer something a little calmer? Then go for cocktails at one of the city's finest cocktail bars.

SHORTLISTS

CLUBS

De School
DR. JAN VAN BREEMENSTRAAT 1,
DESCHOOLAMSTERDAM.NL

MADAM
OVERHOEKSPLEIN 1, ADAMTOREN.NL

Radion
LOUWESWEG 1, RADIONAMSTERDAM.NL

Disco Dolly
HANDBOOGSTRAAT 11, DISCODOLLY.NL

Warehouse Elementenstraat
ELEMENTENSTRAAT 25, ELEMENTENSTRAAT.NL

Marktkantine
JAN VAN GALENSTRAAT 6, MARKTKANTINE.NL

Canvas
WIBAUTSTRAAT 150 (7E VERDIEPING),
VOLKSHOTEL.NL

COCKTAILS

Hiding in Plain Sight
RAPENBURG 18, HPSAMSTERDAM.COM

Porem
GELDERSEKADE 17, POREMAMSTERDAM.COM

Vesper
VINKENSTRAAT 57, VESPERBAR.NL

Door74
REGULIERSDWARSSTRAAT 74, DOOR-74.COM

Tales & Spirits
LIJNBAANSSTEEG 5-7, TALESANDSPIRITS.COM

Apt.
SINGEL 460, APT.AMSTERDAM

Doka
WIBAUTSTRAAT 150, VOLKSHOTEL.NL

24/48/72
HOURS IN

There's so much to discover in Amsterdam that the chances are you'll run out of time. Especially if it's your first visit. Which is why we offer inspiration for making the most of 1, 2 or 3-day visits to Amsterdam. With some classics that you should see at least once, surprising tips and unmissable hotspots.

@YOURLBB

24 HOURS IN AMSTERDAM

In Amsterdam for a layover or a fun day out? Start your day in De Pijp, do something cultural and go from hotspot to hotspot. Today, Tour 2, which begins on the Gerard Doustraat.

9 A.M. breakfast

De Wasserette in cosy De Pijp has for years been one of the nicest spots for a good breakfast. They open early, offer delicious coffee and their menu lists lots of tasty sandwiches.
DE WASSERETTE, EERSTE VAN DER HELSTSTRAAT 27, DEWASSERETTE.COM

10 A.M. Gerard Doustraat

Gerard Doustraat is De Pijp's hipster street, lined with beautiful concept stores and specialty shops.
GERARD DOUSTRAAT

11 A.M. Albert Cuyp Market

A stroll through De Pijp is incomplete without a visit to the Albert Cuyp market, where the most delicious syrup waffles in Amsterdam are sold.

11:30 A.M. lunch

You can enjoy tasty and healthy dishes at CT coffee & coconuts, and it's one of Amsterdam's most beautiful hotspots.
CT COFFEE & COCONUTS, CEINTUURBAAN 282-284, CTAMSTERDAM.NL

1 P.M. museum

Close to De Pijp is the Museumplein, with Amsterdam's three iconic museums: the Rijksmuseum, the Stedelijk Museum and the Van Gogh Museum. Go see an exhibition that suits your taste.
• RIJKSMUSEUM, MUSEUMSTRAAT 1, RIJKSMUSEUM.NL
• STEDELIJK MUSEUM, MUSEUMPLEIN 10, STEDELIJK.NL
• VAN GOGH MUSEUM, MUSEUMPLEIN 6, VANGOGHMUSEUM.NL

9 A.M. Breakfast | 10 A.M. Gerard Doustraat | 11 A.M. Albert Cuyp Market | 11.30 A.M. Lunch

Take a taxi (9 minutes) or walk (20 minutes) via the Spiegelstraat and Prinsengracht to the Runstraat in the Nine Streets. From there we continue Tour 5 in the Canal District and the Nine Streets.

3 P.M. The Nine Streets

The cosy Nine Streets connects the Prinsengracht and the Singel, and is a mecca for those who love specialty stores. Here you'll find the flagship stores of beautiful brands, vintage shops and concept stores, surrounded by with coffee and lunch spots. For a coffee break we recommend the Reestraat, where you'll find Pluck and Ree7, among others.

DE9STRAATJES.AMSTERDAM

5 P.M. drinks

The Hoxton's lobby isn't only for hotel guests. The interior and vibe give you the feeling of being not in Amsterdam, but Brooklyn (NY). It's a nice spot for a drink, around the corner from the Nine Streets and close to the Jordaan.

THE HOXTON AMSTERDAM, HERENGRACHT 255, THEHOXTON.COM

7 P.M. early dinner

There's no shortage of good restaurants in Amsterdam. And it is of course much more fun to eat at a hidden gem than at a restaurant you could easily have found without this guide. Here, therefore, are suggestions for four restaurants where you are guaranteed a fine evening. Each very different from the rest, but all with great service and delicious food.

- SALMUERA, ROZENGRACHT 106-H, SALMUERA.NL
- DE LUWTE, LELIEGRACHT 26, RESTAURANTDELUWTE.NL
- TALES & SPIRITS, LIJNBAANSSTEEG 5, TALESANDSPIRITS.COM
- CAFÉ DE KLEPEL, PRINSENSTRAAT 22, CAFEDEKLEPEL.NL

AFTER DINNER

Still fancy a cocktail after dinner? Then go to Vesper around the corner of the Haarlemmerstraat.

VESPER, VINKENSTRAAT 57, VESPERBAR.NL

24/48/72 HOURS IN

1 P.M.	3 P.M.		5 P.M.	7 P.M.	
Museum	The Nine Streets		Drinks	Early dinner	

48
HOURS

48 HOURS IN AMSTERDAM

On Day 1, follow the first '24 hours in Amsterdam'. Start today with Tour 1 in Amsterdam East's Javastraat and discover the city's most up-and-coming neighbourhood. Tip: Rent a bike to go from one hotspot to the next. We're going from East to West.

9 A.M. breakfast

You can pop in early for a delicious breakfast at Bar Basquiat. It's hotspots like these that are making Javastraat the place to be in East. Order coffee, fresh juice and one of their egg dishes, such as the Shakshuka.

BAR BASQUIAT, JAVASTRAAT 88-90, BARBASQUIAT.NL

10 A.M. Javastraat

We start a part of Tour 1 after breakfast. You'll find a host of fun concept stores, coffee bars and restaurants in the area around Javastraat.

11 A.M. Dapper Market

Cross the Dapper Market in the direction of the Oosterpark. The multicultural Dapper Market is always busy.

11:10 A.M. Tropenmuseum

The Tropenmuseum in Amsterdam East is known for its good, frequently changing exhibitions.

TROPENMUSEUM, LINNAEUSSTRAAT 2, TROPENMUSEUM.NL

12 P.M. Oosterpark

Stroll through the beautiful Oosterpark to the Beukenplein.

12:10 P.M. Coffee Bru

The Beukenplein has changed in recent years into a cosy square with lots of eateries. Bar Bukowski is a nice place to have a drink, but for the best coffee go to Coffee Bru.

COFFEE BRU, BEUKENPLEIN 14 H, COFFEEBRU.NL

9 A.M.	10 A.M.	11 A.M.	11.10 A.M.	12 P.M.
Breakfast	Javastraat	Dapper market	Tropenmuseum	Oosterpark

Grab your bike and cycle via Mauritskade and Nassaukade to The Foodhallen. Or take Tram 3 from the tram stop at Beukenweg and alight at Bilderdijkstraat / Kinkerstraat.

1:15 P.M. The Foodhallen

Food lovers can indulge at The Foodhallen. This indoor food market occupies an old tram depot. It's always super-busy in the evenings, but you can enjoy a relaxed and extended lunch here. Tip: share as many dishes as possible so you can sample more. And make sure you also try something from Viêt View!

DE FOODHALLEN, BELLAMYPLEIN 51, FOODHALLEN.NL

3 P.M. Amsterdam-West

On Tour 3 you will discover the best hotspots in Amsterdam West and De Baarsjes. Explore the area and you'll understand why Amsterdammers are so fond of the West.

5:30 P.M. drinks

One of the nicest drinking spots on the edge of West and the centre is Waterkant. If the weather's good, relax at this tropical hotspot by the water and watch the boats sail by. The Surinamese-flavoured bar snacks are good here. As are the beers!

WATERKANT, MARNIXSTRAAT 246, WATERKANTAMSTERDAM.NL

7:30 P.M. dinner

Amsterdam West is full of nice restaurants, from affordable eateries to cosy gastropubs. You can find them all in the district overview, but to make choosing easier, here are tips for three places you really shouldn't miss:

- PANACHE, TEN KATESTRAAT 117, CAFEPANACHE.NL
- HAPPYHAPPYJOYJOY, BILDERDIJKSTRAAT 158-HS, HAPPYHAPPYJOYJOY.ASIA
- FA. SPEIJKERVET, ADMIRAAL DE RUYTERWEG 79, SPEIJKERVET.NL

AFTER DINNER

If you're in the mood after dinner, you can go clubbing until the early hours. Check the venue schedules to see which DJs are playing!

- DE SCHOOL, DR. JAN VAN BREEMENSTRAAT 1, DESCHOOLAMSTERDAM.NL
- RADION, LOUWESWEG 1, RADIONAMSTERDAM.NL

12.10 P.M. Coffee Bru **1.15 P.M.** The Foodhallen **3 P.M.** Amsterdam West **5.30 P.M.** Drinks **7.30 P.M.** Dinner

72
HOURS

72 HOURS IN AMSTERDAM

Best rent a bike again today. Start the day with breakfast in the Red Light District, and afterwards discover Amsterdam's hidden art and rugged Amsterdam North.

9:30 A.M. breakfast

Go to Gartine for an organic breakfast. This hidden gem is tucked away in a side street off the busy Kalverstraat.

GARTINE, TAKSTEEG 7, GARTINE.NL

11 A.M. Street Art Tour

At weekends you can book a street-art tour of the city centre via Street Art Amsterdam. Street-art fanatic Nicole takes you on a tour of the hidden works of art in the Jordaan and along the canals. Because street art is constantly changing in terms of locations, the start and end points of the tour also change regularly.

STREETARTEUROPE.COM/STREET-ART-
AMSTERDAM-TOUR
(ON SATURDAYS ONLY)

1:45 P.M. lunch

Vinnies is a lovely spot for lunch in the centre. Everything's organic, and the sandwiches are tasty. They have two locations, so check to see which is closest to the end of the Street Art Tour.

VINNIES, NIEUWE ZIJDSKOLK 33-HS &
HAARLEMMERSTRAAT 46, VINNIESHOMEPAGE.COM

After lunch grab your bike and head for Amsterdam North (Tour 6). From behind Central Station, take the free ferry to Buiksloterweg. You're allowed to take your bike on the ferry.

3:30 P.M. Lookout

The best views overlooking Amsterdam are to be had from A'DAM, the tall tower next to the EYE Film Museum. It also

9.30 A.M.	11 A.M.		1.45 P.M.	
Breakfast	Street Art Tour		Lunch	

TIP!
After dinner, go see a movie at
the Filmhallen or The Movies.

houses a hotel, a club and a restaurant.
From the Lookout you have a panoramic
view of the historic centre. Daredevils
can have themselves strapped to a swing
that oscillates over the edge of the
observation deck.

LOOKOUT, OVERHOEKSPLEIN 1, ADAMTOREN.NL

*Cycle to NDSM Wharf. This is without doubt
one of the rawest parts of Amsterdam, and a
popular site for summer festivals.*

5:30 P.M. drinks

Pllek is a popular spot on NDSM Warf.
With its city beach, it's the perfect place
to relax in the summer months. But it's
also always fun inside the hangar!

PLLEK, TT NEVERITAWEG 59, PLLEK.NL

*After drinks, it's time to return to the other
side of the IJ. From NDSM Wharf grab the
ferry back to Central Station.*

7:30 P.M. dinner

Some very good restaurants have opened
in the city centre in the past few years.
It is recommended that for your last day
in Amsterdam you reserve a table at one
of these gems for a wonderful farewell
dinner.

- ARTDELI, ROKIN 93, ART-DELI.COM
- GIN NEO BISTRO & WINES, WESTERSTRAAT 264, GINAMSTERDAM.COM
- CHOUX, DE RUIJTERKADE 128, CHOUX.NL
- KAAGMAN & KORTEKAAS, SINT NICOLAASSTRAAT 43, KAAGMANENKORTEKAAS.NL

3.30 P.M.
Lookout

5.30 P.M.
Drinks

7.30 P.M.
Dinner

EAST

Amsterdam East has undergone a radical transformation in the past five years. From multicultural district with the Dapper Market as its beating heart to hipster neighbourhood with one hotspot after the other opening its doors. It has beautiful parks, like the Oosterpark and Frankendael Park, surrounded by stately buildings and lively food markets. But the district is also home to the raw Wibautstraat, the Beukenplein with its abundance of terraces, trendy Javastraat and the up-and-coming Czaar Peterstraat. It is this diversity that makes Amsterdam East so popular with locals.

BUCKET LIST

19 Oosterpark

Oosterpark is East Amsterdammers' back garden. The park has recently undergone renovations, and it is now a lovely place for a stroll, a picnic or a jog. There are lots of cosy neighbourhood cafés near the Oosterpark, as is the Tropenmuseum.

24 Tropenmuseum

The Tropenmuseum is devoted to world cultures and is housed in a magnificent building on the edge of the Oosterpark. A *must* not only for the changing exhibitions that comment on the current zeitgeist, but also because of the museum's lovely café. The terrace of the Grand Café De Tropen on the balcony of the museum is a must in the summer.

LINNAEUSSTRAAT 2, TROPENMUSEUM.NL, 088-0042800, TRAM: 9 – EERSTE VAN SWINDENSTRAAT

5 Canvas & de Volkshotel rooftop

You could probably count Amsterdam's rooftop terraces on one hand, but they're certainly worth visiting for a bit of that New York feeling. When in East, check out the hip Volkshotel, where you can sleep, work, eat and club. Canvas restaurant is on the seventh floor, and offers not only tasty food, but also fantastic views of the city below from its roof terrace.

WIBAUTSTRAAT 150, VOLKSHOTEL.NL, 020-2612110, METRO: 51, 53 & 54 – WIBAUTSTRAAT, TRAM: 3 – WIBAUTSTRAAT/RUYSCHSTRAAT

25 Javastraat

The trendy Javastraat is one of the nicest streets in East. This part of the East is also called the East-Indian neighbourhood. You'll find many authentic local shops here, with products from all around the world. Alongside the Turkish greengrocer you will now also find nice coffee bars, fine restaurants, cosy cafés to drink in and concept stores.

8 Park Frankendael & Pure Markt

Once a city nursery providing Amsterdammers with fresh vegetables, now a beautiful park where you can enjoy a lovely stroll. In the park stands Amsterdam's only remaining country estate: Huize Frankendael. After your walk, you can enjoy a drink here in the Merkelbach restaurant. The park hosts regular events, including the Pure Markt, which takes place almost every month on Sunday – the place to be for traditional food and a culinary afternoon.

HUIZEFRANKENDAEL.NL, PUREMARKT.NL

EAST

TOUR 1

1. BOTERHAM
2. BETER & LEUK
3. STEK
4. RESTAURANT C
5. CANVAS & DE VOLKS-HOTEL ROOFTOP
6. RIJSEL
7. DE VERGULDEN EENHOORN
8. PARK FRANKENDAEL & PURE MARKT
9. BIGGLES
10. &KLEVERING
11. BAR WISSE
12. HET FAIRE OOSTEN
13. MICHEL-INN
14. OLIVES & MORE
15. THULL'S
16. EDDY SPAGHETTI
17. COFFEE BRU
18. BAR BUKOWSKI
19. OOSTERPARK
20. ALL THE LUCK IN THE WORLD

21. WE ARE VINTAGE
22. DE BIERTUIN
23. LOUIE LOUIE
24. TROPENMUSEUM
25. JAVASTRAAT
26. DIV. HERENKABINET
27. HARTJE OOST
28. BEDFORD STUYVESANT
29. BAR GALLIZIA
30. THE WALTER WOODBURY BAR
31. BAR BASQUIAT
32. NELIS
33. DRAAGBAAR
34. DIV. DAMESBOUDOIR
35. WILDE ZWIJNEN & EET-BAR WILDE ZWIJNEN
36. KEF
37. CP113
38. MAGAZIN
39. WORSCHT
40. AMSTERDAM ROEST

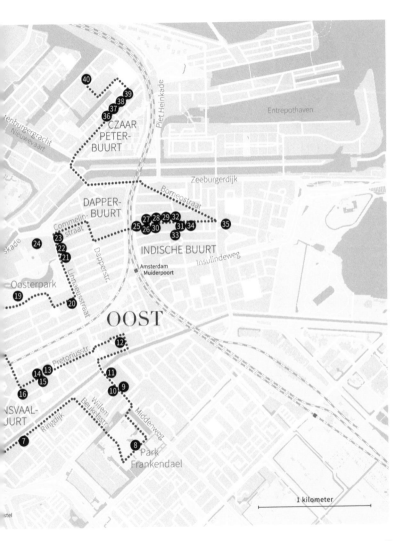

EAST

1 kilometer

FOOD& DRINK

TIP!
Book a table in advance to secure your spot at the fashionable restaurants.

23 LOUIE LOUIE

Housed in a beautiful large building overlooking the Oosterpark and offering a warm welcome from early morning till late evening, Louie Louie is the living room of the East for breakfast, lunch or just a coffee or drinks. The menu is inspired by Latin American cuisine. The volume of the music typically goes up a notch as evening becomes night.

LINNAEUSSTRAAT 13, LOUIELOUIE.NL, TRAM: 9 – EERSTE VAN SWINDENSTRAAT

6 RIJSEL

Rijsel is jam-packed every night of the week. Which isn't surprising, since here it's all about pure and authentic food inspired by French cuisine. The menu changes frequently and always includes delicious three-course options. This unique restaurant, with its huge open kitchen and vintage furniture, is located in a former domestic science school. Reservations are a must!

MARCUSSTRAAT 52, RIJSEL.COM, 020-4632142, TRAM: 3 – WIBAUTSTRAAT/ RUYSCHSTRAAT, TRAM: 12 – STATION AMSTERDAM AMSTEL, METRO: 51, 53 & 54 – WIBAUTSTRAAT

3 STEK

If you're looking for a nice spot for breakfast or lunch, go to Stek on the Wibautstraat. Don't be put off by the building's somewhat ugly exterior. Inside it's both cosy and industrial: sturdy wooden tables, wild flowers in vases, and old school chairs. The menu offers a variety of sandwiches, salads and soups, and Stek also serves drinks at weekends.

WIBAUTSTRAAT 95, STEK-AMSTERDAM.COM, METRO: 51, 53, & 54 – WIBAUTSTRAAT, TRAM: 3 – WIBAUTSTRAAT/RUYSCHSTRAAT

.Rijsel

Bar Bukowski

11 BAR WISSE

You can spend the entire day at Bar Wisse on the Linneauskade, from early morning until late at night. With its cheerful blue façade, this is a bar where you feel at home immediately and can get a good meal anytime of the day. The wall mural and beautiful bar are quite eye-catching. In summertime Bar Wisse has a terrace next to the water.

LINNAEUSKADE 1A, 020-2219228, TRAM: 9 – HOGE WEG OR PRETORIUSSTRAAT

18 BAR BUKOWSKI

There are all sorts of food and drink spots on the Beukenplein in East and Bar Bukowski is one of the favourites. A quintessential all-day hotspot, open from breakfast-time until late at night. This cosy café serves delicious Flammkuchen,

boasts a sunny terrace during the summer months, and at weekends one area becomes Henry's Bar, where you can order and enjoy delicious cocktails!

OOSTERPARK 10, BARBUKOWSKI.NL, 020-3701685, TRAM: 3 & 7 – BEUKENWEG

17 COFFEE BRU

For the best coffee in the up-and-coming Beukenplein, go to Coffee Bru. It's cosy inside, so chances are you'll be staying for more than one coffee. Light wood, lots of green plants and a small terrace in the summer. They serve the most delicious cakes to go with the coffee, such as the Red Velvet Cake. You can also have breakfast and lunch here.

BEUKENPLEIN 14, COFFEEBRU.NL, 020-7519956, TRAM: 3 & 7 – BEUKENWEG

Boterham

1 BOTERHAM

Boterham is a hidden gem near the Wibautstraat and is a fun place for both coffee and shopping. You're welcome for breakfast and lunch (with organic toppings), or to score beautiful home accessories. There's a good chance you won't be able to keep your eyes off the shelving unit where the nicest items are displayed.

ANDREAS BONNSTRAAT 2, 020-6631842, METRO: 51, 53 & 54 – WEESPERPLEIN, TRAM: 3 – CAMPERSTRAAT

40 AMSTERDAM ROEST

When the weather's good, you'll find Amsterdammers at one of the city beaches. Amsterdam Roest is an eatery, bar, city beach and creative hub in one, located on the waterfront in an old industrial area full of warehouses and factories. Keep an eye on its programme, as they often have cool events.

JACOB BONTIUSPLAATS 1, AMSTERDAMROEST.NL, 020-3080283, TRAM: 10 – EERSTE LEEGHWATER-STRAAT

7 THE VERGULDEN EENHOORN

This former town farm on the Ringdijk has been transformed into a restaurant and bar. Be warned: once seated, you won't want to leave. The Vergulden Eenhoorn is an oasis of calm in the middle of the city. They serve delicious dishes all day long, from lunch- to dinner-time in the picnic garden or in the restaurant that was formerly a cowshed.

RINGDIJK 58, VERGULDENEENHOORN.NL, 020-2149333, METRO: 51, 53 & 54: STATION AMSTERDAM AMSTEL, TRAM: 12 – STATION AMSTERDAM AMSTEL

The Vergulden Eenhoorn

2 BETER & LEUK

Beter & Leuk is a super-healthy hotspot just around the corner of the Wibautstraat. In fact almost everything on the menu is vegetarian, vegan or gluten-free! The interior with its vintage furnishing feels as cosy as a living room, and delicious-looking cakes adorn the counter. In addition to enjoying your meal, you can also shop for items from Things I Like, Things I Love, among other brands.

EERSTE OOSTERPARKSTRAAT 91, BETERENLEUK.NL, 020-7670029, METRO: 51, 53 & 54 – WIBAUTSTRAAT, TRAM: 3 – WIBAUTSTRAAT/RUYSCHSTRAAT

22 DE BIERTUIN

Opposite the Oosterpark is De Biertuin, a perfect spot for drinks and dinner. The food here is good (you *must* try the spit-roasted

TIP!
No budget for a full-course dinner? You can dine very affordably at the eateries in East.

chicken) and also very affordable. As the name suggests, the food here revolves around beer. The craft beer list is extensive, and includes some by Amsterdam brewers. The terrace with beer tables is heated, and this is a good place to bask in the sun once the first rays hit.

LINNAEUSSTRAAT 29, DEBIERTUIN.NL, 020-6650956, TRAM: 9 – EERSTE VAN SWINDENSTRAAT

32 NELIS

Tucked away in a side street off the trendy Javastraat is Nelis, a cosy neighbourhood café that's perfect for those occasions when you're not in the mood for anything elaborate. You get a good bite here at a reasonable price. It's the sort of classic eatery that every neighbourhood ought to have. When the weather's good, you can enjoy it in the hidden courtyard.

SUMATRASTRAAT 28, NELISAMSTERDAM.NL, 020-2211642, TRAM: 7 – MOLUKKENSTRAAT

Beter & Leuk

Eddie Spaghetti

31 BAR BASQUIAT

With a 7.30 A.M. weekday opening time, this is the ultimate spot for breakfast on the Javastraat. Start the day with a coffee at Bar Basquiat (they make great coffee) and order one of their egg dishes to go with it. The lunch menu offers various sandwiches and Lebanese pizzas, which are so delicious that it's wise to share with friends so you get to taste more than one. This is the place to be later in the evening for drinks and enough bar snacks to pass for dinner.

JAVASTRAAT 88, BARBASQUIAT.NL, TRAM: 14 – JAVAPLEIN

16 EDDY SPAGHETTI

Eddy Spaghetti serves the most delicious pastas in East. You'll find this Italian bistro with its beautiful wood parquet floors and marble tables in a corner building on the Krugerplein. There are various primi on the menu that are perfect for sharing, pizzas and well-filled pastas. Before your meal, have an aperitivo at the bar, just like the Italians do!

KRUGERPLEIN 23, EDDYSPAGHETTI.NL, 020-3709388, METRO: 51, 53 & 54 – WIBAUTSTRAAT

35 WILDE ZWIJNEN

Lovers of good and pure food couldn't be any happier than in East! You can enjoy an extended dinner at the Wilde Zwijnen restaurant on the Javaplein, or smaller dishes at Eetbar Wilde Zwijnen. The menu offers Mediterranean meat and fish dishes with local ingredients. Both spots share a rugged yet warm décor.

JAVAPLEIN 23, WILDEZWIJNEN.COM, 020-4633043, TRAM: 14 – JAVAPLEIN

Wilde Zwijnen

Bedford Stuyvesant

28 BEDFORD STUYVESANT

If you're in the mood for coffee on the Javastraat, then Bedford Stuyvesant is a must. This coffee bar is inspired by Bedford–Stuyvesant in Brooklyn, New York. Besides good coffee, this American coffee bar also serves fresh juices and breakfast! Tip: After-hours pop-up dinners happen here often.

JAVASTRAAT 55, BEDFORDSTUYVESANT.NL, 020-3342175, TRAM: 7 – MUIDERPOORTSTATION, TRAM: 14 – JAVAPLEIN

30 THE WALTER WOODBURY BAR

Regulars refer affectionately to this bar as 'Walter's'. This all-day hotspot was one of the first eateries to open on the Javastraat for which even West Amsterdammers hopped on their bikes. The Walter Woodbury Bar is open for coffee, lunch, dinner and drinks. The G&T list is pretty extensive,

making this a fine place for a late drink.

JAVASTRAAT 42, WALTERWOODBURYBAR.NL, 020-2333021, TRAM: 7 – MUIDERPOORTSTATION

13 MICHEL-INN

It's quite likely that no one had heard of Steve Bikoplein until a few years ago, not until Michel-Inn opened its doors. From delicious pizzas prepared in a wood oven to culinary pinchos and tapas, all the dishes are perfect for sharing. After dinner, on goes the vinyl, and you're free to linger with a cocktail while playing a traditional Dutch board game.

STEVE BIKOPLEIN 12, MICHEL-INN.NL, 020-7370673, TRAM: 9 – PRETORIUSSTRAAT, METRO: 51, 53 & 54 – WIBAUTSTRAAT

29 BAR GALLIZIA

Being at Bar Gallizia gives you the feeling of joining an Italian family. Everything here is done the Italian way, from a good espresso in the morning to focaccia for lunch. This spot on the Javastraat stays open all day, and serves only the finest Italian cuisine. A lovely place to sip wine late in the afternoon, with a side plate of antipasti.

JAVASTRAAT 67, GALLIZIA.NL, 020-3706204,
TRAM: 7 – MUIDERPOORTSTATION,
TRAM: 14 – JAVAPLEIN

4 RESTAURANT C

Food at the tastefully decorated restaurant C is based on a very special concept. Here it's all about degrees Celsius. Small dishes are offered and presented on the menu according to the various temperatures at which they were cooked: from -20 to 200 degrees Celsius. Want to taste a bit of everything? Then order the 360-degree menu! The C also stands for cocktails, so start your dining experience with an aperitif.

WIBAUTSTRAAT 125, C.AMSTERDAM, 020-2103011,
METRO: 51, 53 & 54 – WIBAUTSTRAAT, TRAM: 3 –
WIBAUTSTRAAT/RUYSCHSTRAAT

EAST

Restaurant C

SHOPPING

TIP!
Fill up a picnic basket with goodies from Kef and Worscht and visit the Oosterpark.

27 HARTJE OOST

Hartje Oost revolves around two things: great coffee and interesting brands. Have breakfast or lunch here and choose from a selection of homemade dishes prepared with local ingredients, wherever possible. Then shop in the store for the latest must-haves. You'll find a well-curated collection at this store on the Javastraat, from fashion to accessories and from vintage to self-designed items.

JAVASTRAAT 23, HARTJEOOST.NL, 020-2332137, TRAM: 7 – MOLUKKENSTRAAT

33 DRAAGBAAR

Nowadays as you walk through Javastraat, you should also check out the side streets. On the Sumatrastraat you'll find Draagbaar, a concept store: shop and hair salon under one roof. They only work with organic products in the salon, leaving your hair silky smooth. The store is stocked with beautiful products from up-and-coming designers, including many from Amsterdam.

SUMATRASTRAAT 54, DRAAGBAAR.NU, TRAM: 7 – MOLUKKENSTRAAT

15 THULL'S

The term 'Amsterdam pickles' is truly honoured at Thull's in Pretoriusstraat. It's all about pickles at this unique food shop: pickled vegetables of all kinds. The lunch menu has a long list of specialty sandwiches with authentic toppings that you don't often see anymore on Amsterdam menus. And that's what makes Thull's such a nice hidden gem. Tip: You can also order everything to go, from evening meals to homemade preserves for the pantry.

PRETORIUSSTRAAT 69, THULLS.NL, 020-3635474, TRAM: 7 – BEUKENWEG

Thull's

Hartje Oost

10 &KLEVERING

Those who love shopping for beautiful home accessories should remember the name &Klevering. Here you'll find the most original items that are always on trend. This store has several branches in town, and the one in East is on the Middenweg. Those looking for a special gift, new crockery or home accessories have come to the right place.

MIDDENWEG 38, KLEVERING.NL,
020-3637354, TRAM: 9 – HOGEWEG

37 CP113

At concept store CP113, named after the abbreviation of the street name and the address number, you'll find everything collected under one roof. This is where to shop for trendy brand-name clothes, curated from around the world. But you can also buy vintage items and fun accessories. And did we mention that you can unwind here over a cup of coffee, too?

CZAAR PETERSTRAAT 113, CP113.COM, 020-2231976,
TRAM: 14 – PONTANUSSTRAAT, TRAM: 10 – EERSTE
LEEGHWATERSTRAAT

12 HET FAIRE OOSTEN

Het Faire Oosten (The Fair East) is a shop and art gallery in one. Great for home accessories, clothing and personal care products. But better yet, almost everything here is locally made and fair trade. Exhibitions are held a few times a year in the gallery section, with artworks on sale at affordable prices.

WALDENLAAN 208, HETFAIREOOSTEN.NL,
TRAM: 7 – LINNAEUSSTRAAT/WIJTTENBACHSTRAAT

Biggles

9 BIGGLES

More and more nice shops are opening on the Middenweg. At Biggles everything revolves around fashion and lifestyle. You can shop here for home items, from ceramic and glass vases to cushion covers with trendy prints. But they also have a good fashion collection for men and women, from basics that everyone should have in their wardrobe to items that'll give your wardrobe a fashion-season update.

MIDDENWEG 55A, BIGGLESFASHION.COM, 020-7520102, TRAM: 9 – HOGEWEG

38 MAGAZIN

Magazin could best be described as a mini department store. This concept store is a platform for local artists and artisans and stocks mostly fair-trade products, from scarves to crockery and sustainably produced items for the home.

CZAAR PETERSTRAAT 139, MAGAZINAM STERDAM.NL, TRAM: 10 – EERSTE LEEGH-WATERSTRAAT

TIP!
&Klevering also has a store at Jacob Obrecht-straat 19a and another at Haarlemmer-straat 8.

14 OLIVES & MORE

It's love at first sight at shops like Olives & More. It's got a bright interior with lots of light wood, and a large table through which an olive tree grows. As the name suggests, this is *the* address for the best olives. What began as an operation selling at local markets and out of a cargo bike has become a store from which you can buy the best olives and olive oils. They organise regular tastings and you can sign up every month to join a table d'hote dinner.

PRETORIUSSTRAAT 68D, OLIVESANDMORE.NL, TRAM: 7 – LINNAEUSSTRAAT/WIJTTENBACHSTRAAT

EAST

Olives & More

36 KEF

For the best cheese in Amsterdam you need to go to Abraham Kef. Having begun with one location on the Marnixstraat, they're now also to be found in East. Cheese specialist Abraham Kef stocks a wonderful selection of French cheeses, matching wines and real French baguettes. Lovely to eat at home, but also to sample on the spot during cheese and wine tastings.

CZAAR PETERSTRAAT 137, ABRAHAMKEF.NL
020-4207873, TRAM: 14 – PONTANUSSTRAAT

TIP!
All the Luck in the World is my go-to store for unique gifts.

39 WORSCHT

Where at Kef on the Czaar Peterstraat everything revolves around cheese, Worscht is the place for, well, sausages. Not just your usual sausages, but artisanal sausages from the best suppliers. To complete the culinary experience, true sausage lovers also shop here for their knives, sturdy cutting boards, pickles, ketchup and mustard.

CZAAR PETERSTRAAT 153, WORSCHT.NL
TRAM: 10 – EERSTE LEEGHWATERSTRAAT

21 WE ARE VINTAGE

We Are Vintage is a large vintage store within walking distance of the Dapper Market. Those who love vintage should definitely take a look. New items for men and women are added every week and properly sorted. On the counter sits a huge weighing scale (also vintage!), as you pay for your finds by the kilo.

EERSTE VAN SWINDENSTRAAT 2,
WEAREVINTAGE.NL, 020-7852777,
TRAM: 9 – EERSTE VAN SWINDENSTRAAT

All the Luck in the World

26-34 DIV. HERENKABINET & DAMESBOUDOIR

DIV has not one but two locations on the Javastraat: one for men, the Herenkabinet, and one for ladies, the Damesboudoir. You can shop at both stores for urban-style clothes and gadgets from around the world, from Japanese denim to Swedish backpacks. And sneakers, lots and lots of sneakers!

- HERENKABINET: JAVASTRAAT 8, 020-694408, TRAM: 3 – MUIDERPOORTSTATION

- DAMESBOUDOIR: JAVASTRAAT 100, 020-3418387, TRAM: 7 – MOLUKKENSTRAAT

DIVAMSTERDAM.COM

20 ALL THE LUCK IN THE WORLD

The concept store All the Luck in the World might just become your favourite shop. They sell trendy jewellery and such beautiful notebooks and home accessories that you might find yourself becoming greedy. Must-haves for ladies and kids, but also vintage furniture from French flea markets refurbished for a new home.

LINNAEUSSTRAAT 20, ALLTHELUCKINTHEWORLD.NL, TRAM: 7 – LINNAEUSSTRAAT/WIJTTENBACHSTRAAT

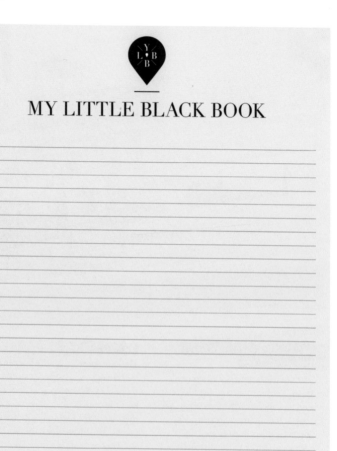

MY LITTLE BLACK BOOK

_____
_____
_____
_____
_____
_____
_____
_____
_____
_____
_____
_____
_____
_____
_____
_____
_____
_____
_____
_____
_____
_____
_____
_____
_____
_____
_____
_____

NOTES

DE PIJP

DE PIJP

Ferdinand Bolstraat

Once a working class area, now one of Amsterdam's hippest neighbourhoods. Until about ten years ago, De Pijp was mostly populated by students, but now everyone comes to drink in its cosy cafés. Surrounded by terraces and lovely concept stores, the Albert Cuyp market has always been the district's beating heart. The hip Gerard Doustraat is not to be missed. As are the Ceintuurbaan, Van Woustraat and Ferdinand Bolstraat, which have all been transformed in recent years.

26 Gerard Douplein and -street

Gerard Doustraat is *the* street for unique concept stores, and is not to be missed. This is where you'll find the coolest fashion shops, concept stores and boutiques. For lunch and drinks, go to one of the hotspots on the Gerard Douplein, where the terraces are open all year round, just like in Paris.

17 Brouwerij Troost (Pub-brewery)

Brouwerij Troost occupies a former monastery on the Cornelius Troostplein. With views onto the enormous vats in which the beers are brewed, this is *the* place for a craft beer tasting session in De Pijp. Sample a variety of miniature specialty beers and order a tasty snack to go with it. This pub-brewery also serves good food!

CORNELIS TROOSTPLEIN 21, BROUWERIJTROOST-DEPIJP.NL, 020-7371028, TRAM: 12 – CORNELIS TROOSTPLEIN

23 Albert Cuyp Market & streetfood

The most famous market in Amsterdam is hard to miss in De Pijp. You can buy almost anything here, from affordable vegetables to fabrics and the tastiest street food. The freshly baked syrup waffles are the best to be had in Amsterdam! This vibrant market is open Monday to Saturday from 9am to 5pm. You'll find even more nice eateries hidden behind the market stalls, all of which you could walk past without noticing during the day.

24 Speakeasy cocktailbar The Butcher

Whereas in New York, London or Tel Aviv, there are speakeasy cocktail bars on almost every corner, in Amsterdam you can count them on one hand. All the more reason to visit this one in the Albert Cuyp. Burgers in the front, cocktails at the back. Find out the password (or reserve a place at The Butcher's "Secret" Kitchen) and walk past the cold room to the stylishly equipped secret kitchen for some tasty nibbles and cocktails. Reservations can be made only via hello@the-butcher.com.

ALBERT CUYPSTRAAT 129, THE-BUTCHER.COM, 020-4707875, TRAM: 16 & 24 – ALBERT CUYPSTRAAT

9 Sarphatipark

Sarphatipark isn't large, but it is beautiful. It's a park where you don't have to wade through a sea of tourists, and where locals come to picnic and enjoy the sun. The eye-catchingly beautiful fountain is a national monument. Worth noting: barbecuing is not permitted in the Sarphatipark, unfortunately, so treat yourself to something from one of the many nearby specialty food stores.

TOUR 2

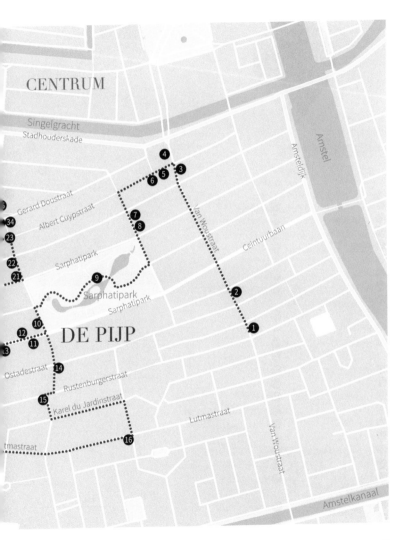

CENTRUM

Singelgracht
Stadhouderskade

Gerard Doustraat

Albert Cuypstraat

Sarphatipark

Sarphatipark
Sarphatipark

DE PIJP

Ostadestraat

Rustenburgerstraat

Karel du Jardinstraat

Lutmastraat

...tmastraat

Amstelkanaal

Jan Woustraat

Ceintuurbaan

Amstel

Amsteldijk

Van Woustraat

FOOD& DRINK

TIP!
Equally crazy about Vietnamese summer rolls? Then Pho 91 is a must.

34 DE WASSERETTE

De Wasserette is a breakfast, lunch and brunch classic in De Pijp, and is already open by 7.30 in the morning. You can enjoy the best sandwiches here, with a variety of fillings, and all-day dishes like eggs Benedict. But even if all you want is coffee, we recommend this café on the corner of the Gerard Douplein. Don't be surprised if you have to wait for a table at weekends.

EERSTE VAN DER HELSTSTRAAT 27, DEWASSERETTE.COM, TRAM: 16 & 24 – ALBERT CUYPSTRAAT

25 PHO 91

Pho 91 is a Vietnamese eatery along the Albert Cuyp market, with vintage furniture, plants in wooden crates and drawings on the wall. The menu consists of authentic and healthy Vietnamese street food made according to old family recipes. Start the evening with the small dishes, which are perfect for sharing. For the main course, order a pho (noodle soup) or a bun (noodle salad) with vegetables and meat or fish.

ALBERT CUYPSTRAAT 91, PHO91.NL, 020-7526880, TRAM: 16 & 24 – ALBERT CUYPSTRAAT

40 CANNIBALE ROYALE

If you're a meat lover, be sure to visit Cannibale Royale on the Ruysdaelkade. At this extraordinary brasserie, you get the best quality meats for lunch or dinner. Don't expect haute cuisine, just good ingredients and solid dishes, from steaks to burgers and spareribs. Light eaters can choose from a range of salads. Tip: they also have a branch in the city centre, where you can eat until well after midnight.

RUYSDAELKADE 149, CANNIBALEROYALE.NL, 020-2335860, TRAM: 16 & 24 – RUYSDAELSTRAAT

De Wasserette

Brut de Mer

33 BRUT DE MER

For oysters and bubbly, you must visit Brut de Mer on the Gerard Douplein. Whatever you want to call it, oyster bar, seafood restaurant, the fact is you get nothing here but the best seafood from Zeeland. Lovely spot for savouring a plate of oysters and a good glass of wine after shopping. The place and its interior make you feel like you're in a small brasserie in Paris. Order a plateau of fruit de mer in the evening, or the Côte de Poisson for two. Nice for a romantic dinner à deux.

GERARD DOUPLEIN 8, 020-4714099, BRUTDEMER.NL, TRAM: 16 & 24 – ALBERT CUYPSTRAAT

7 LITTLE COLLINS

Little Collins is a tribute to Melbourne (Australia), where you can go for a boozy brunch from Wednesday to Sunday. It serves classic brunch dishes with an international twist, in which eggs play a central role, and dishes from around the world made for sharing with the whole table. This eatery in a side street off the Albert Cuypstraat is also open for dinner from Thursday to Saturday. Tip: Order a Bloody Mary to go with your meal. They're possibly the best in town!

EERSTE SWEELINCKSTRAAT 19F, LITTLECOLLINS.NL, 020-6732292, TRAM: 4 – CEINTUURBAAN/VAN WOUSTRAAT

Geflipt Burgers

18 VOLT

Volt gastropub on the Ferdinand Bolstraat is a perfect spot for a meal and drink. A popular neighbourhood eatery that's pleasantly crowded every night of the week. The menu changes frequently, but always retains a couple of classics, such as the octopus dish and the bavette. Try one of the specialty beers from the extensive beer list. They also have a nice terrace here in the summer.

FERDINAND BOLSTRAAT 178, RESTAURANTVOLT.NL, 020-4715544, TRAM: 3 & 12 – CEINTUURBAAN/ FERDINAND BOLSTRAAT

12 SLA

Sla's interior is to die for. You can find this hip and, above all, very healthy salad bar at various locations in the city. But the one on the Ceintuurbaan is where it all began.

Create your own salad or choose one of the salads of the season. Delectable and healthy. Devour on the spot or order to go.

CEINTUURBAAN 149, ILOVESLA.COM, 020-7893080, TRAM: 3 – TWEEDE VAN DER HELSTSTRAAT

3 GEFLIPT BURGERS

Not in the mood for anything elaborate? Then go for a burger at Geflipt Burgers. They serve organic burgers – beef, chicken or vegetarian, with side dishes like french fries and coleslaw. There's a large sunny terrace in the summer months, and it's nice and warm inside at the wooden tables in the colder seasons. Grab a window seat so you can people-watch on the busy Van Woustraat.

VAN WOUSTRAAT 15, GEFLIPTBURGERS.NL, 020-4714590, TRAM: 4 – STADHOUDERSKADE

Sla

15 SIR HUMMUS

Hummus, originally from the Middle East, is now a staple part of Dutch cuisine. But for authentic hummus made from honest ingredients, go to Sir Hummus. They serve a variety of hummus with pita bread and salad at this small eatery on the Van der Helstplein, all healthy and creamy, just the way you want it. Get here early, because it takes 24 hours to prepare hummus, and once they run out, they're out.

VAN DER HELSTPLEIN 2, SIRHUMMUS.NL, 020-6647055, TRAM: 3 – TWEEDE VAN DER HELSTSTRAAT

TIP!
From Thursday to Saturday evening, Gerard Douplein is the place to be for drinks in De Pijp.

35 BAR MASH

Where to hangout for drinks and appetizing snacks. Bar Mash is a tiny bar with a striking interior on the Gerard Douplein. The whole place is panelled with particleboard, and lit by incandescent bulbs hanging above the bar. Simple and all the nicer for it. Not that you'll spend a lot of time admiring the interior – it's packed in the evenings with hipsters listening to old school hip-hop. The terrace in summer with its long beer tables is highly recommended.

GERARD DOUPLEIN 9, TRAM: 16 & 24 – ALBERT CUYPSTRAAT

37 BAKERS & ROASTERS

Bakers & Roasters is one of the most cheerful coffee bars in De Pijp. The best of New Zealand and Brazil is combined here, from coffee to homemade pies. The delicious breakfast burritos, egg dishes and pastries are prepared in an open kitchen. Pop in for all-day breakfast or brunch, and order a fresh smoothie, juice or cocktail to go with it.

EERSTE JACOB VAN CAMPENSTRAAT 54, BAKERSANDROASTERS.COM, TRAM: 16 & 24 – STADHOUDERSKADE

Sir Hummus

Fa. Pekelhaaring

1 FA. PEKELHAARING

The Italian restaurant Fa. Pekelhaaring is a popular spot in De Pijp. Not only because they serve delicious, contemporary Italian cuisine at affordable prices, but also because the place is furnished with a nice mix of vintage and design elements, lending it an incredibly cosy feel.

VAN WOUSTRAAT 127-129, 020-6790460, PEKELHAARING.NL, TRAM: 4 – LUTMASTRAAT

19 CT COFFEE & COCONUTS

CT coffee & coconuts is housed in a former 1920s cinema. What was once the Ceintuur Theater is now one of the city's most beautiful spots. Covering no less than four floors and fitted out by Sukha concept store with furniture in beautiful natural colours, hanging plants and lots of wood, this is where hip Amsterdam goes for breakfast and stays late for good coffee and tasty food. Tip: Order the fresh coconut milk and imagine yourself on a tropical island.

CEINTUURBAAN 282-284, CTAMSTERDAM.NL, 020-3541104, TRAM: 3 & 12 – CEINTUURBAAN/ FERDINAND BOLSTRAAT

14 GLOUGLOU

Glouglou wine bar serves over forty natural wines, in other words organic wines with no artificial additives. Savour nature in all its purity at this spot on the corner of Tweede van der Helststraat. Order a cheese or meat platter to go with your wine and you have the perfect drinking scenario. Did we mention that all the wines are available to go?

TWEEDE VAN DER HELSTSTRAAT 3, GLOUGLOU.NL, TRAM: 3 – TWEEDE VAN DER HELSTSTRAAT

Paskamer

11 SINNE

For a culinary evening, Sinne on the Ceintuurbaan is a must. This Michelin-starred restaurant serves classic French/Mediterranean dishes at surprisingly good prices. You can get a divine three-course meal here for € 35. It looks like an ordinary neighbourhood restaurant but the food is extraordinarily high quality. We recommend making reservations.

CEINTUURBAAN 342, RESTAURANTSINNE.NL, 020-6827290, TRAM: 3 – TWEEDE VAN DER HELSTSTRAAT

6 CALLE OCHO

More and more nice restaurants are opening on the Albert Cuypstraat. At Calle Ocho you're in for Miami style street food: salsas and platos with a Latin American flavour. All dishes are made for sharing, so you get to taste as many flavours as possible. Order a cocktail with Cuban rum to go with it and your night is complete.

ALBERT CUYPSTRAAT 226, CALLE-OCHO.NL, 020-3638077, TRAM: 4 – STADHOUDERSKADE

10 SCANDINAVIAN EMBASSY

This beautiful, coolly furnished Scandinavian hotspot is a favourite among coffee lovers. They serve specialty coffees from the best Nordic coffee roasters. You can order a healthy breakfast to go with your coffee, or brunch/lunch (with a Scandinavian twist) made with organic local ingredients. Coffees are also to go.

SARPHATIPARK 34, SCANDINAVIANEMBASSY.NL, TRAM: 3 – TWEEDE VAN DER HELSTSTRAAT

5 DE JAPANNER

De Japanner is hidden behind a couple of market stalls on the Albert Cuyp. It's a Japanese restaurant that feels like an Amsterdam pub with a varied Japanese menu of classics like sushi, gyoza and tempura, all made with fresh ingredients straight from the market. Goes down nicely with a Japanese beer! Tip: a good place for late night dining, too.

ALBERT CUYPSTRAAT 228, DEJAPANNER.COM, 020-2339939, TRAM: 4 – STADHOUDERSKADE

TIP!
Grab a coffee at the Scandinavian Embassy then stroll through the beautiful Sarphatipark.

16 PASKAMER

The Paskamer (fitting room) lies midway between the Van Woustraat and the Ferdinand Bolstraat. A café and tasting room with a nice homey atmosphere, thanks to the friendly host. The menu lists small dishes from different world cuisines: great for sharing! They also have an extensive cocktail menu with perfect "fits" to go with your meal.

LUTMASTRAAT 132, 020-3627468, PASKAMER.NU, TRAM: 4 – LUTMASTRAAT

DE PIJP

36 DIM SUM NOW

Dim sum is the new sushi, and for tasty steamed dumplings and gyoza in De Pijp, go to Dim Sum Now. A cheerfully decorated eatery with a range of dim sum dishes for lunch or dinner, or to go.

FERDINAND BOLSTRAAT 36, DIMSUMNOW.COM, TRAM: 16 & 24 – ALBERT CUYPSTRAAT & STADHOUDERSKADE

Dim Sum Now

SHOPPING

TIP!
Eerste van der Helststraat and Gerard Doustraat are the shopping streets in De Pijp.

22 SETS

If you're not paying attention, you'll walk right past Sets, because this shop is in one of those typical Amsterdam buildings with a super-narrow façade. This small concept store for ladies sells clothes in lovely neutral colours, organic beauty products, and silver jewellery made by the shop's owner.

EERSTE VAN DER HELSTSTRAAT 74, 020-3642708, TRAM: 16 & 24 – ALBERT CUYPSTRAAT

31 ANNA + NINA

Anne + Nina is a cool concept store on the Gerard Doustraat that you must not miss if you're in De Pijp. A "candy" store filled with beautiful clothing, jewellery (including brands like Catbird from New York) and items for the home. This is a perfect store for shopping for that special gift for yourself or a friend.

GERARD DOUSTRAAT 94, ANNA-NINA.NL, 020-2044532, TRAM: 16 & 24 – ALBERT CUYPSTRAAT

39 KOLIFLEUR

Kolifleur concept store is a hidden gem near the Ferdinand Bolstraat. It's unlikely you'd stumble upon it if you didn't already know it was there. They sell second-hand clothes by contemporary fashion designers like Isabel Marant and Acne. But you can also find beautiful vintage furniture from the fifties and sixties and score leather goods and jewellery by Dutch designers. A nice mix of vintage and designer items!

FRANS HALSSTRAAT 35, KOLIFLEUR.NL, TRAM: 16 & 24 – STADHOUDERSKADE

Kolifleur

Charlie + Mary

probably find what you want at Het Kaufhaus.

EERSTE SWEELINCKSTRAAT 21, HETKAUFHAUS.NL, TRAM: 4 – CEINTUURBAAN/VAN WOUSTRAAT

38 MUMU VITAMIN CHOCOLATES

Mumu Vitamin Chocolates is a chocolate-addict's paradise. The chocolates at this shop in De Pijp are pure, natural *and* healthy. The Mumus are actually enriched with vitamins, and taste divine. You can indulge your sweet tooth here without guilt!

EERSTE JACOB VAN CAMPENSTRAAT 33, MUMUVITAMINCHOCOLATES.COM, TRAM: 16 & 24 – STADHOUDERSKADE

29 CHARLIE + MARY

Anyone who's socially conscious about fashion should definitely not miss Charlie + Mary on the Gerard Doustraat. You'll find only fair-trade and sustainable brands here, each with a special story that'll make you appreciate the items even more. Besides clothing for fashionable men and women, you'll find a selection of books, jewellery and other must-haves.

GERARD DOUSTRAAT 84, CHARLIEMARY.COM, 020-6628281, TRAM: 16 & 24 – ALBERT CUYPSTRAAT

8 HET KAUFHAUS VINTAGE

This lovely vintage store in De Pijp sells clothing and accessories, furniture, home accessories and vinyl records. In terms of clothing, think trendy, wearable basics. And at affordable prices! In search of a Persian rug, unique chair or table? You'll

Anna + Nina

Yay

28 YAY

It's all about a healthy lifestyle at Yay, with a shop, café and workshops under one roof. You can shop for fair trade and sustainable products, tuck into the tastiest raw-food dishes in the café (you definitely shouldn't miss the cakes!) or take a yoga class. All are possible at Yay, with entrances on the Albert Cuypstraat *and* Gerard Doustraat.

GERARD DOUSTRAAT 74,
YAYAMSTERDAM.NL, TRAM: 16 & 24 –
ALBERT CUYPSTRAAT

TIP!
Pick a hotspot on this page for something healthy.

20 NINOUR

You'll find shop and deli Ninour on a quiet side street off the Ferdinand Bolstraat. A concept store where you can also have a delicious breakfast or lunch. The menu offers healthy dishes with a Moroccan twist. That is if you ever make it to the cheerful pink café area, as there's a good chance you'll be distracted on your way by their lovely collection of desirable items for ladies, kids, and the home.

EERSTE JAN STEENSTRAAT 109,
NINOUR.NL, TRAM: 16 & 24 – ALBERT
CUYPSTRAAT

21 COTTONCAKE

The Cottoncake concept store is a breakfast spot and shop in one. The two owners travel the world to find the most gorgeous clothes and special must-haves. The exquisite interior is almost all white, with some dark wood and black accents. A lovely spot for an organic breakfast or brunch, or just a coffee if you're visiting the Albert Cuyp market.

EERSTE VAN DER HELSTRAAT 76,
COTTONCAKE.NL, 020-7895838,
TRAM: 16 & 24 – ALBERT CUYPSTRAAT

DE PIJP

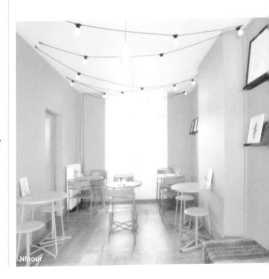
Ninour

Cottoncake

2 GATHERSHOP

Everything in this little concept store on the Van Woustraat is handmade, each item with a unique design and a story about the designer. The shop's interior is as beautiful as the products it sells, which include jewellery, postcards, clothing and leather accessories. Nothing here is mass-produced.

VAN WOUSTRAAT 99, GATHERSHOP.NL, 020-7520681, TRAM: 4 – CEINTUURBAAN/ VAN WOUSTRAAT

TIP!
After shopping, stroll through the Albert Cuyp market and treat yourself to a freshly baked syrup waffle. So yummy…

32 BASKÈTS

Real sneaker fan? Then don't miss Baskèts in De Pijp. You can shop here for sneakers, but also for urban clothing for men and women, and for books and gadgets. You'll find brands from all around the world, forming an exclusive street-style collection.

GERARD DOUSTRAAT 96, BASKETS-STORE.COM, 020-4701010, TRAM: 16 & 24 – ALBERT CUYPSTRAAT

4 HUTSPOT

Hutspot is the largest and perhaps most beautiful concept store in Amsterdam. With branches on both the Rozengracht and in De Pijp, you can spend hours poking around for something special. They stock a well-curated collection of clothes for ladies and gents, and gadgets to crave. There's seating space for lunch or coffee on the first floor, which is nice, and Bar Hutspot is right next door for evening time.

VAN WOUSTRAAT 4, HUTSPOTAMSTERDAM.COM, 020-2231331, TRAM: 4 – STADHOUDERSKADE

Felice

Hutspot

30 FELICE

Felice operates on the 'fast fashion' concept. Their collection changes every week, so you discover new things with every visit. Ladies and gents can shop here for sophisticated clothes, shoes, handmade leather bags and items for the home from established brands and up-and-coming designers and artists.

GERARD DOUSTRAAT 88,
FELICEHOMEOFBRANDS.COM,
TRAM: 16 & 24 – ALBERT CUYPSTRAAT

13 NOBODY HAS TO KNOW

Familiar with unisex fashion? Nobody Has To Know sells clothes that can be worn by both men and women. You'll find timeless classics here by the store's own label: NHTK. Also worth knowing: all the clothes are made in a small workshop right here in Amsterdam. It doesn't get any more local than that.

CEINTUURBAAN 320, NOBODYHASTOKNOW.COM,
TRAM: 3 – CEINTUURBAAN/FERDINAND BOLSTRAAT

27 THE FRAGRANCE STORE

In search of a unique scent? Then visit The Fragrance Store, where they'll help you find one that matches your style and personality. This perfume boutique specialises in hard-to-find fragrances from original and not yet mainstream perfumeries from around the world, fragrances with scents you're not likely to smell on anyone else.

GERARD DOUSTRAAT 72, THEFRAGRANCESTORE.NL,
020-7606232, TRAM: 16 & 24 – ALBERT CUYPSTRAAT

MY LITTLE BLACK BOOK

AMSTERDAM
WEST
& DE BAARSJES

Waterkant

Amsterdam West is a neighbourhood with families from different cultures and hipsters living side by side. Trendy eateries and concept stores alternate with phone shops and international restaurants. The most up-and-coming part of West is De Baarsjes, long a district for which no one made a detour, but now with hotspots popping up all over the place like mushrooms.

BUCKET LIST

18 The Foodhallen

This used to be an old tram depot in West, but was transformed into a complex with shops, restaurants and an indoor food market called The Foodhallen. The stalls sell small dishes that are perfect for sharing with friends while enjoying a drink at the bar.

BELLAMYPLEIN 51, FOODHALLEN.NL, TRAM: 7 & 17 – TEN KATEMARKT

11 Waterkant

Waterkant is an unusual summer hotspot on the waterfront (unusual in that it's built underneath a multi-storied parking garage), with an interior inspired by Paramaribo in Surinam. Expect a relaxed atmosphere, Surinamese beers and a menu with a long list of tropical treats.

MARNIXSTRAAT 246, WATERKANTAMSTERDAM.NL, 020-7371126, TRAM: 7 & 10 – ELANDSGRACHT

1 Jan Pieter Heijestraat

The Jan Pieter Heijestraat in Amsterdam West is rapidly developing and has become the nicest street in its neighbourhood. You'll find unique boutiques like Gesponnen Suiker, concept stores like Johnny at the Spot, and a variety of eateries like Voldaan.

40 Marktkantine

Marktkantine (market canteen) is a creative pop-up in Amsterdam West: a theatre, club and restaurant under one roof. Go for the vintage markets or to dance until the early hours. But first grab a bite at the Graceland B-B-Q, a typical American roadhouse restaurant serving barrel-smoked dishes. Check the schedule to see which DJs are playing.

JAN VAN GALENSTRAAT 6, MARKTKANTINE.NL, 020-7231760, TRAM: 3 – HUGO DE GROOTPLEIN

20 The Filmhallen

You'll find The Filmhallen right next to The Foodhallen. It's the sister cinema to The Movies, the oldest cinema in Amsterdam's Haarlemmerbuurt. This unique cinema screens the latest movies and documentaries, and is housed in a former tram depot in the Ten Katebuurt.

HANNIE DANKBAARPASSAGE 12, FILMHALLEN.NL, 020-8208122, TRAM: 7 & 17 – TEN KATESTRAAT

AMSTERDAM-
WEST
& DE BAARSJES

TOUR 3

1 JAN PIETER HEIJESTRAAT

2 JOHNNY AT THE SPOT

3 GESPONNEN SUIKER

4 VOLDAAN

5 MASHED

6 FRIDAY NEXT

7 TEDS

8 JUTKA EN RISKA

9 T'S BITES AND WINE

10 MARVIN

11 WATERKANT

12 SALAD AND THE CITY

13 HAPPYHAPPYJOYJOY

14 WILDERNIS

15 LOT SIXTY ONE

16 CAFÉ PANACHE

17 THE LOCAL GOODS STORE

18 THE FOODHALLEN

19 VIÊT VIEW

20 THE FILMHALLEN

21 BRASSERIE HALTE 3

22 THE BREAKFAST CLUB

23 BAR BROUW

24 SPAGHETTERIA

25 BERRY

26 MOOK

27 T.I.T.S.

28 ROTISSERIE AMSTERDAM

29 MISC STORE

30 BAR SPEK

31 FA. SPEIJKERVET

32 HET HUYSRAAT

33 VAN ONS

34 RADIJS

35 BAR BAARSCH

36 THINGS I LIKE, THINGS I LOVE

37 HET MASSAGEHUYS

38 WHITE LABEL COFFEE

39 TOON

40 MARKTKANTINE

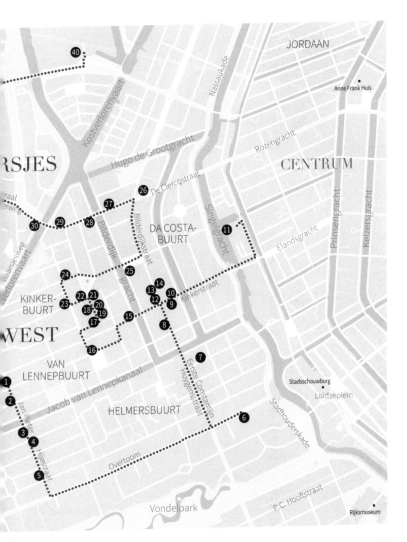

JORDAAN

Anne Frank Huis

RSJES

Kostverlorenvaart

Hugo de Grootgracht

Rozengracht

CENTRUM

Prinsengracht

Keizersgracht

De Clercqstraat

40

raal
nerweg

30 29 28 27 26

Bilderdijkstraat

Bilderdijk

DA COSTA-
BUURT

Singelgracht

Elandsgracht

11

Bilderdijkkade

dwarsstraat
erlorenvaart

24

25

gracht

14
13

10
12
9

Linnaeusstraat

KINKER-
BUURT

22 21
18 20
19
17

23

15

8

WEST

16

7

Eerste Constantijn
Huygensstraat

VAN
LENNEPBUURT

1

Jacob van Lennepkanaal

2

Jan Pieter

3

4

Heijestraat

HELMERSBUURT

Stadsschouwburg

Leidseplein

Stadhouderskade

6

5

Overtoom

Vondelpark

P.C. Hooftstraat

Rijksmuseum

FOOD& DRINK

TIP!
There are loads of good restaurants in De Hallen, or you could just grab a quick bite at one of the food stalls.

19 VIÊT VIEW

Viêt View is without doubt one of the best food stands in The Foodhallen. This is where to get mouth-watering Vietnamese street food like bánh mì and summer rolls. If there's a queue at dinner-time, it's more than worth the wait.

HANNIE DANKBAARPASSAGE 16, VIETVIEW.NL, TRAM: 7 & 17 – TEN KATEMARKT

31 FA. SPEIJKERVET

Fa. Speijkervet is a popular restaurant in an old bakery in De Baarsjes. It's got a basic brasserie-style interior, but a very surprising menu with artisanal dishes. Cooking here abides by the 'from head to tail' principle whereby no part of the animal is wasted.

ADMIRAAL DE RUIJTERWEG 79, SPEIJKERVET.NL, 020-2236004, TRAM: 7 – JAN EVERTSENSTRAAT/DE WITH, TRAM: 12 & 13 – ADMIRAAL DE RUIJTERWEG

24 SPAGHETTERIA

Within walking distance of De Hallen is a food paradise for pasta lovers. Spaghetteria pasta bar is a nice spot for an affordable bite, offering a choice of six fresh, homemade pastas: two each of fish, meat and veg. Classics, all, with that authentic Italian taste.

JAN HANZENSTRAAT 32, SPAGHETTERIA-PASTABAR.NL, TRAM: 7 & 17 – TEN KATESTRAAT

Fa. Speijkervet

Brasserie Halte 3

21 BRASSERIE HALTE 3

You'll find several restaurants next to the food stands in De Hallen, including Remise47, Meat West and Brasserie Halte 3. The last of these serves gastropub-style dishes in a beautiful interior. Pure, tasty and affordable. After dinner, have a drink at the Gin & Tonic Bar in De Hallen.

BELLAMYPLEIN 51, HALTE3.NL, 020-2181775, TRAM: 7 & 17 – TEN KATESTRAAT

38 WHITE LABEL COFFEE

Coffee lovers regard White Label Coffee as one of the best specialty coffee bars in town. It's all about quality here, from production to the moment you taste the coffee. Ask the friendly baristas for advice, and feel right at home in the bright wood-furnished interior. Tip: Order the homemade apple pie to go with your coffee!

JAN EVERTSENSTRAAT 136, WHITELABELCOFFEE.NL, 020-7371359, TRAM: 7 & 13 – MERCATORPLEIN

22 THE BREAKFAST CLUB

For breakfast all day, go West to The Breakfast Club, popular for its buckwheat pancakes, juices, coffee and homemade granola. Enjoy breakfast in its bright and cosy interior in a building on a corner of the Bellamyplein.

BELLAMYSTRAAT 2, THEBREAKFASTCLUB.NL, TRAM: 7 & 17 – TEN KATESTRAAT

Bar Spek

12 SALAD AND THE CITY

Salad and the City on the Bilderdijkstraat is one of the nicest healthy-eating hotspots in West. A takeaway and delivery salad bar with a bright interior accented in green and black. And the salads? These feature surprising combinations, and are super-healthy, of course.

BILDERDIJKSTRAAT 164, SALADANDTHECITY.NL, 020-2333241, TRAM: 3 & 12 – BILDERDIJKSTRAAT/ KINKERSTRAAT

23 BAR BROUW

Bar Brouw is for lovers of artisanal meats and craft beer. This eatery namely serves smoked meats, such as spareribs, burgers, brisket and pulled pork. The blue interior with brass accents is both cosy and rugged, and the prices affordable.

TEN KATESTRAAT 16, BARBROUW.NL, 020-2238569, TRAM: 7 & 17 – TEN KATESTRAAT

30 BAR SPEK

Bar Spek is a good place for a drink with friends. This cosy café on the Admiraal De Ruijterweg has a vintage-style industrial interior, and a terrace next to the water for the summer months. It's also quite pleasant indoors when the temperature drops.

ADMIRAAL DE RUIJTERWEG 1, BARSPEK.NL, 020-6188102, TRAM: 7 – JAN EVERTSENSTRAAT/DE WITH, TRAM: 12, 13 & 14 – WILLEM DE ZWIJGERLAAN

Salad and the City

16 CAFÉ PANACHE

Café Panache is in a former market storage facility around the corner from the Ten Kate Market. This hotspot has a rugged urban yet chic interior, and is a good spot for an extended dinner with friends. You can even order the cocktails in pitchers, the better for sharing. The restaurant becomes a popular bar in the evenings. Petit Panache is Café Panache's smaller brother, and occupies the porch area; it's a good spot for dim sum and a drink with friends.

TEN KATESTRAAT 117, CAFEPANACHE.NL, 020-2211736, TRAM: 7 & 17 – TEN KATESTRAAT

TIP!
Lots of great brunch spots in Amsterdam West, for example TEDS. More brunch tips on pages 28-29.

4 VOLDAAN

You can enjoy a healthy home-cooked meal in the hip rural interior of Voldaan on the Jan Pieter Heijestraat. A great spot for lunch or a quick bite in the evening. They serve healthy seasonal comfort food, such as soup with homemade meatballs. Also recommended for vegetarians!

JAN PIETER HEIJESTRAAT 121, FACEBOOK.COM/VOLDAAN.AMSTERDAM, TRAM: 1 & 17 – JAN PIETER HEIJESTRAAT

7 TEDS

TEDS is perfect for early birds. This breakfast and brunch spot opens at 7 in the morning. Grab a place on the chesterfield and make yourself at home. This hotspot serves tasty egg dishes and sandwiches all day. The "spirited high tea" featuring cocktails instead of tea is recommended.

BOSBOOM TOUSSAINTSTRAAT 60, 020-3627396, TEDS-PLACE.NL, TRAM: 7 & 17 – BILDERDIJKSTRAAT, TRAM: 3 & 12 – BILDERDIJKSTRAAT/KINKERSTRAAT

Café Panache

Happyhappyjoyjoy

35 BAR BAARSCH

You'll find the all-day hotspot Bar Baarsch near the Mercatorplein, in the heart of De Baarsjes. A favourite for years for lunch, drinks and dinner. They serve top-quality pub food here, prepared on a charcoal grill, and very affordable it is, too. The interior is hip and modern.

JAN EVERTSENSTRAAT 91, BARBAARSCH.NL, 020-6181970, TRAM: 7 & 13 – MERCATORPLEIN

13 HAPPYHAPPYJOYJOY

Those who love dim sum and other Asian dishes will feel right at home at Happyhappyjoyjoy. This hotspot's menu is packed with street food from Vietnam, Thailand, Indonesia and the like. With its cheerful interior bedecked with neon letters, Asian posters and geisha umbrellas, you'll forget you're still in Amsterdam.

BILDERDIJKSTRAAT 158, HAPPYHAPPYJOYJOY.ASIA, 020-3446433, TRAM: 3 & 12 – BILDERDIJKSTRAAT/ KINKERSTRAAT

9 T'S BITES AND WINE

T's Bites and Wine is a great place for a drink at the end of the day. It's the sort of wine bar where you stick around for a bite. The wine list at this lovely place is international, and the small culinary dishes on the menu are perfect for sharing. Tip: You can also go for a wine tasting at T's.

KINKERSTRAAT 53, TS-LIFESTYLE.NL, 020-2219391, TRAM: 3 & 12 – BILDERDIJKSTRAAT/KINKERSTRAAT, TRAM: 7 & 17 – TEN KATESTRAAT

Berry

25 BERRY

Being at Berry is like having a coffee
in a cosy living room. A great place for
breakfast, lunch and homemade cake. The
chalkboard menu above the bar lists the
day's treats. Order the breakfast deluxe for
breakfast or a sandwich for lunch. Have a
coffee with it and you're sorted!

BILDERDIJKKADE 27, BERRYAMSTERDAM.NL,
020-3707300, TRAM: 3 & 12 – BILDERDIJKSTRAAT/
KINKERSTRAAT

28 ROTISSERIE AMSTERDAM

Rotisserie Amsterdam has been packed
every day since it opened. Not surprising,
as this New York inspired bar and grill on
the De Clercqstraat looks pretty awesome.
They serve tender spit-roasted chicken and
juicy burgers, and delicious cocktails at
weekends.

DE CLERCQSTRAAT 81, ROTISSERIEAMSTERDAM.NL,
020-2217918, TRAM: 3 & 12 – BILDERDIJKSTRAAT/
KINKERSTRAAT

Rotisserie Amsterdam

15 LOT SIXTY ONE

Lot Sixty One has made a name for itself in Amsterdam with its coffee. This popular coffee bar is tiny, so not a place to linger over coffee for hours. But your coffee will be made with professional care and knowledge. Tip: go on a Monday or Tuesday when the beans are roasted and savour the wonderful aroma.

KINKERSTRAAT 112,
LOTSIXTYONECOFFEE.COM, TRAM: 3, 7, 12 & 17 – BILDERDIJKSTRAAT/KINKERSTRAAT

26 MOOK

Everything revolves around pancakes at Mook. Not your regular pancakes, but healthy pancakes from breakfast to dinnertime. Order sweet or savoury along with a fresh juice. Men get special consideration with a real "mancake", which features bacon.

DE CLERCQSTRAAT 34, TRAM: 3, 12, 13 & 14 – BILDERDIJKSTRAAT

TIP!
Must-not-miss streets in West: De Clercqstraat, Jan Pieter Heijestraat, Bilderdijkstraat, Admiraal De Ruyterweg and Jan Evertsenstraat.

34 RADIJS

The Radijs café was one of the first hotspots on the Jan Evertsenstraat in De Baarsjes. It's a popular neighbourhood spot for breakfast and drinks with friends. During the day you'll find freelancers working on their MacBooks in its sturdy wood-dominated interior. The terrace on the Admiralengracht is great for people-watching.

JAN EVERTSENSTRAAT 41,
RADIJS-AMSTERDAM.NL, 020-7513232, TRAM: 7 & 13 – MARCO POLOSTRAAT

AMSTERDAM WEST

Radijs

SHOPPING

TIP!
The Baarsjes is the up-and-coming part of Amsterdam West, with lots of boutiques.

6 FRIDAY NEXT

Friday Next is a concept store on the Overtoom. A furniture shop where you can also have lunch, drink coffee and work, selling designs and nice must-haves by established names and emerging talent. The homemade quiche is a must for lunch.

OVERTOOM 31, FRIDAYNEXT.COM, 020-6123292, TRAM: 1 – EERSTE CONSTANTIJN HUYGENSSTRAAT, TRAM: 3 & 12 – OVERTOOM

37 HET MASSAGEHUYS

You can unwind at Het Massagehuys in De Baarsjes, just a few doors from White Label Coffee. This hotspot is proof that an authentic massage salon doesn't have to look shabby. But make no mistake: what's on offer is a range of traditional oriental massages with homemade massage oils that you can also buy for home use. Finish with a pot of organic tea!

JAN EVERTSENSTRAAT 110, MASSAGEHUYS.NL, 020-6123251, TRAM: 7 & 13 – MERCATORPLEIN

3 GESPONNEN SUIKER

Fashion lovers couldn't be any happier at Gesponnen Suiker on the Jan Pieter Heijestraat. The collection of clothing, bags and accessories changes frequently at this unique store. You can buy cool women's clothes for any time of the day here. Also nice: everything is very affordable, too.

JAN PIETER HEIJESTRAAT 114, GESPONNENSUIKER.NL, 020-6160108, TRAM: 1 & 17 – JAN PIETER HEIJESTRAAT

Het Massagehuys

Gesponnen Suiker

17 THE LOCAL GOODS STORE

You'll find nothing but Amsterdam brands at The Local Goods Store. This store originated from the popular Local Goods Market, which takes place every fortnight at De Hallen. Call it what you will – concept store, workshop with products by local producers – the fact is you can score cool and innovative items here.

HANNIE DANKBAARPASSAGE 39,
LOCALGOODSSTORE.NL, 020-6246380,
TRAM: 7 & 17 – TEN KATESTRAAT

36 THINGS I LIKE, THINGS I LOVE

Things I Like, Things I Love is without doubt the favourite of hipster ladies in Amsterdam. You will find a carefully curated collection with a combination of vintage, second-hand, new clothes (including the house brand!) and customized items in the area of fashion, home and lifestyle. All super hip and boho style.

JAN EVERTSENSTRAAT 106,
THINGSILIKETHINGSILOVE.COM, 020-7894344,
TRAM: 7 & 13 – MERCATORPLEIN

113

Jutka en Riska

8 JUTKA EN RISKA

Those who love vintage but aren't keen on rummaging through dusty shelves are in the right place at Riska en Jutka. You'll find well-selected on-trend vintage items next to clothes from their own label and young designers. Equally nice are the crave-worthy and very affordable necklaces, earrings and sunglasses.

BILDERDIJKSTRAAT 194, JUTKAENRISKA.NL, 020-6188021, TRAM: 3 & 12 – BILDERIJKSTRAAT/KINKERSTRAAT

TIP!
Amsterdam is packed with vintage shops like Jutka en Riska. See page 31 for the best tips.

10 MARVIN

The Kinkerstraat is not the most beautiful street in Amsterdam. But gems like the concept store Marvin are adding more and more colour to this gritty street. A deli and gift shop under one roof. Come here for a coffee and a nice lunch and leave with the nicest items for your home, from table linen to cookbooks and crockery.

KINKERSTRAAT 66, MARVIN.AMSTERDAM, 020-8455099, TRAM: 3 & 12 – BILDERDIJK-STRAAT/KINKERSTRAAT

29 MISC STORE

If you love beautiful stationery, then Misc Store in De Baarsjes is *the* place. Notebooks, stationery, pencils and pens and office accessories of extraordinary design. Lots and lots of beautiful things to transform your home office! Or to buy as the perfect gift.

DE CLERCQSTRAAT 130, MISC-STORE.COM, 020-7009855, TRAM: 12, 13 & 14 – WILLEM DE ZWIJGERLAAN

27 T.I.T.S.

Don't let the name scare you off. T.I.T.S. stands for "This Is The Shit". And they're right, because the store is full of edgy fashion items, very fine basics, bold accessories and organic beauty products. Anything you buy here will cheer you up.

DE CLERCQSTRAAT 78, TITS-STORE.COM, TRAM: 3 & 12 – BILDERDIJKSTRAAT

AMSTERDAM WEST

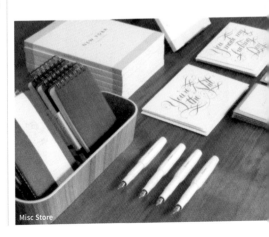

Misc Store

T.I.T.S.

32 HET HUYSRAAT

Had a bite to eat at Radijs? Then go shopping at Huysraat. This design store exudes tranquillity, balance and simplicity, and only sells items that complement each other. It's the sort of place where you become inspired to get your home décor in order.

WITTE DE WITHSTRAAT 182, HETHUYSRAAT.NL, 020-3636958, TRAM: 12, 13 & 14 – ADMIRAAL DE RUIJTERWEG

TIP!
Amsterdam West is a paradise for scoring unique items for the home.

33 VAN ONS

Nothing beats a personalised interior, decorated with unique items you can't find just anywhere. For beautifully restored Dutch and Danish design in Amsterdam, go to Van OnS's showroom. You'll find high quality vintage design furniture and home accessories just waiting for a new home. Tip: they also have a webshop.

WITTE DE WITHSTRAAT 123, VANONS.EU, TRAM: 12, 13 & 14 – ADMIRAAL DE RUIJTERWEG

5 MASHED

Mashed concept store is the sort of shop where you can spend the entire afternoon browsing. They sell the kind of nice things that make you develop a craving. Almost everything here is by Dutch designers, which makes it extra special. Thus local *and* unique!

JAN PIETER HEIJESTRAAT 168, MASHED-CONCEPT-STORE.NL, TRAM: 1 & 17 – JAN PIETER HEIJESTRAAT

Wildernis

14 WILDERNIS

Wildernis is a plant paradise in Amsterdam West. Houseplants hang everywhere in this new-style urban garden shop – plants to enhance your home and balcony, gardening books and lovely plants pots. You're also welcome to have a cup of tea or coffee and a piece of cake here.

BILDERDIJKSTRAAT 165F, 020-7852517, WILDERNISAMSTERDAM.NL, TRAM: 3, 7, 12 & 17 – BILDERDIJKSTRAAT/KINKERSTRAAT

39 TOON

Toon is a unique spot for creative entrepreneurs. An experience store with ateliers and shop-in-shops for artists and entrepreneurs to present their products to the world. The store is decorated with vintage furniture that's also for sale. Order a cup of coffee and explore! There are live music performances as well.

JAN EVERTSENSTRAAT 4, TOON-AMSTERDAM.NL, TRAM: 7 – JAN EVERTSENSTRAAT/DE WITH, TRAM: 12 & 13 – ADMIRAAL DE RUIJTERWEG

2 JOHNNY AT THE SPOT

They sell nothing but beautiful things at Johnny at the Spot. Home accessories, Danish and Swedish fashion (for both men and women), leather bags and shoes. All good quality and on-trend. Tip: don't forget to look around the street corner, where you'll find Johnny's Outlet!

JAN PIETER HEIJESTRAAT 94, JOHNNYATTHESPOT.NL, 020-4893868, TRAM: 1 & 17 – JAN PIETER HEIJESTRAAT

MY LITTLE BLACK BOOK

GO WHERE
YOUR DREAMS
TAKE YOU

JORDAAN
& WESTERPARK

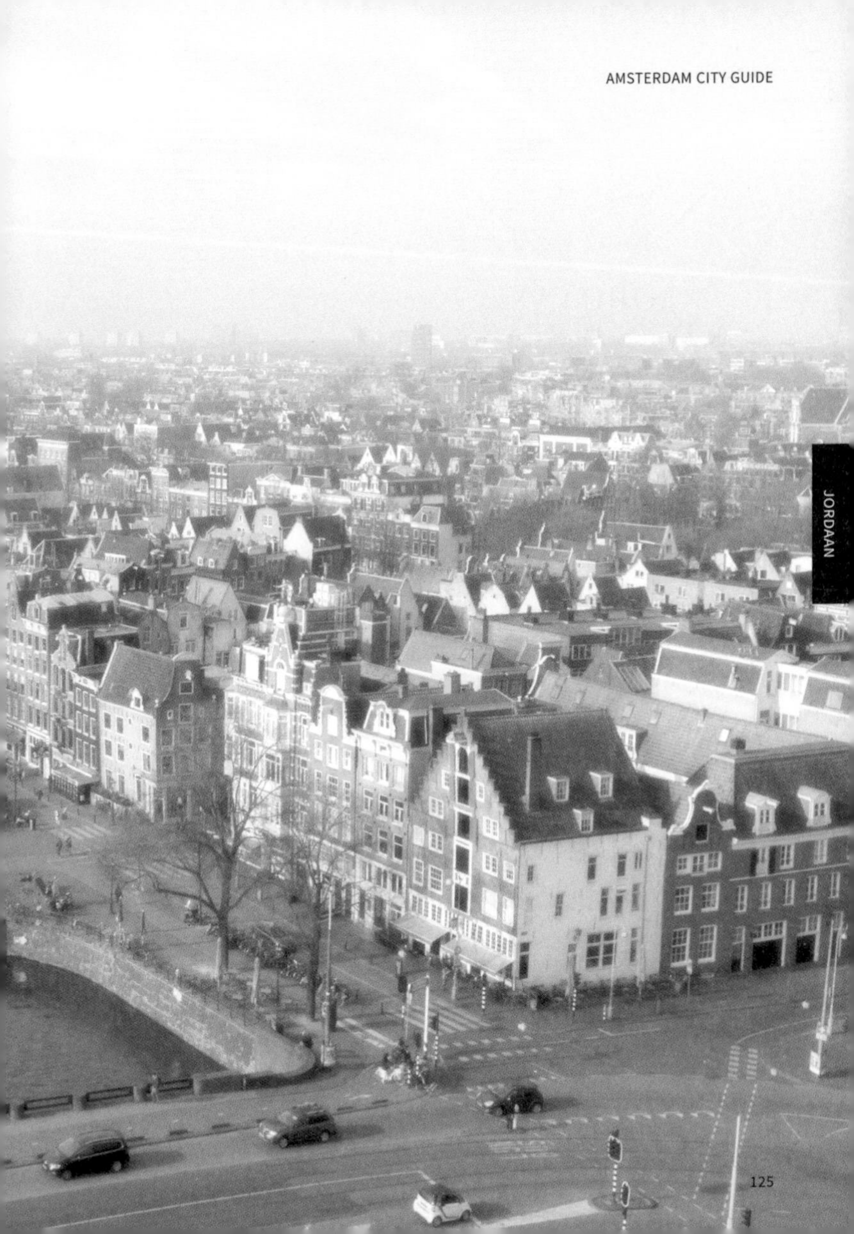

Westergas terrain

To experience the real Amsterdam atmosphere, you must visit the Jordaan. In this cosy working class neighbourhood you'll find traditional brown cafés next to good restaurants and beautiful shops. Go zigzagging through the narrow streets, shop at the boutiques in the Haarlemmerbuurt and relax in the Westerpark. In the old industrial buildings at the Westergas terrain you'll now find numerous restaurants and a cinema.

BUCKET LIST

34 Sunday markets

A lazy Sunday for Amsterdammers means going out for brunch and visiting one of the Sunday markets. At the Westergas terrein you'll find the NeighbourFood Market (for tasty food and vintage items) and the Sunday Market (for art, fashion and design).

WESTERGASTERREIN, NEIGHBOURFOODMARKET.NL, SUNDAYMARKET.NL, TRAM: 10 – VAN HALLSTRAAT

12 Noordermarkt

The Noordermarkt is in the middle of the Jordaan. It's a large open market where a farmers market is held on Saturdays and a vintage market on Mondays. After shopping, go for some apple pie at Winkel 43, still the tastiest in Amsterdam.

NOORDERMARKT, NOORDERMARKT-AMSTERDAM.NL, TRAM: 3 & 10 – MARNIXPLEIN

35 Westerpark

The Westerpark is probably the most popular Amsterdam park among locals, not only because you can have a cosy picnic or barbecue here in the summertime, but also because of the creative enterprises that are now housed in the old industrial halls. There's a cinema and several cafés and restaurants in the Westergasfabriek, with regular events organised both here and in the Westerpark.

JORDAAN

16 Haarlemmerdijk and Haarlemmerstraat

The Haarlemmerdijk and Haarlemmerstraat are the most popular shopping streets in the Jordaan. It's always busy here, and you'll find lots of concept stores, specialty stores, vintage shops and cosy lunch- and coffee bars.

33 Gashouder

Throughout the year, the Gashouder in the Westergas terrein hosts various events like Fashion Week and Unseen, but also festivals and house parties. You too *must* party here at least once. The characteristic building and the huge circular space remain impressive as you dance into the early hours.

KLÖNNEPLEIN 1, WESTERGASFABRIEK.NL, TRAM: 10 – VAN HALLSTRAAT

TOUR 4

1. BALTHAZAR'S KEUKEN
2. SALMUERA
3. LES DEUX FRÈRES
4. SNEAKER DISTRICT
5. KESSENS
6. L'INVITÉ
7. ROBINS HOOD
8. GIN NEO BISTRO & WINES
9. INDIANAWEG10
10. BAR BOCA'S
11. KOEVOET
12. NOORDERMARKT
13. TOSCANINI
14. DAALDER
15. G'S
16. HAARLEMMERDIJK AND HAARLEMMERSTRAAT
17. VINNIES
18. MY-OH-MY
19. TENUE DE NÎMES
20. IBERICUS
21. SUKHA
22. STORE WITHOUT A HOME
23. SIX AND SONS
24. THIS IS HAPPENING
25. RESTORED
26. MARBLES VINTAGE
27. TOKI
28. CONCRETE MATTER
29. DIS
30. KOFFIE ENDE KOECK
31. CAFÉ RESTAURANT AMSTERDAM
32. MOSSEL & GIN
33. GASHOUDER
34. SUNDAY MARKETS
35. WESTERPARK
36. BOCCONI
37. CAFÉ DE WALVIS
38. DOPHERT
39. BAR MICK
40. PIKOTEO

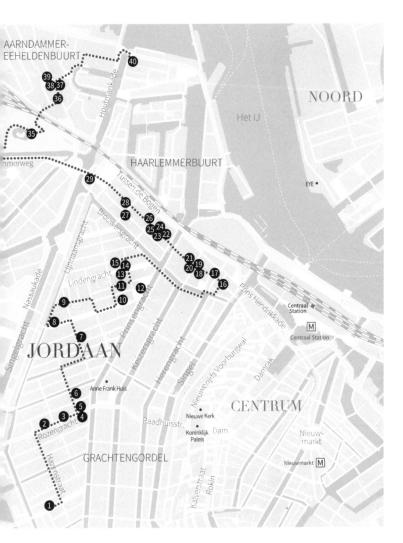

FOOD& DRINK

TIP!
If you go to
Kessens, be
sure to try their
salmon sand-
wich, prepared
the traditional
Swedish way.

17 VINNIES

Vinnies has been a popular breakfast and lunch spot in the Haarlemmerbuurt ever since it opened
its doors. You can enjoy a good
coffee in its homely atmosphere,
and eat healthy dishes like salads
and sandwiches. In addition,
you can actually buy the vintage
furniture you're sitting on.

HAARLEMMERSTRAAT 46, VINNIESHOME
PAGE.COM, 020-2332899, TRAM: 1, 2, 5, 13
& 17 – CENTRAAL STATION WESTZIJDE

11 KOEVOET

You might struggle to make the
connection the first time you walk
into Koevoet. You're supposed
to be at an Italian restaurant,
right? Yet here you are in a
brown Jordanese café where time
appears to have stood still since
the forties. The menu features
classic Italian dishes. No pizzas,
but delicious antipasti, fish and
meat dishes, and a divine burrata
as an eternal special.

LINDENSTRAAT 17, 020-6240846, TRAM: 3
& 10 – MARNIXPLEIN

40 PIKOTEO

An all-day hotspot with a
Spanish touch. You can have
a sandwich at midday, and
pop in later for modern tapas
with an international twist.
Small, beautifully prepared and
presented dishes for sharing with
your table. A bar-restaurant where
you can sit comfortably in the
light-filled conservatory while
enjoying your meal, or have a
cocktail at the bar during a date.

HOUTMANKADE 9, PIKOTEO.NL,
TRAM: 3 – ZOUTKEETSGRACHT

Pikoteo

VINNIES
good home food

EARLY BIRDS
7:30am - 9am
€1 espresso
€2 latte
€2 cappuccino

Vinnies

5 KESSENS

Kessens is a nice breakfast and lunch spot on the Rozengracht. You're welcome from 8.30am on weekdays for coffee and cake, a hearty breakfast and delicious sandwiches. The interior has a Scandinavian touch and is bright and airy, with lots of wood. Also nice: there's a large table at the back where you're welcome to work.

ROZENGRACHT 24, KESSENSAMSTERDAM.NL, 020-2217431, TRAM: 13, 14 & 17 – WESTERMARKT

14 DAALDER

Daalder looks like a very ordinary eatery in the Jordaan, but those who've eaten here know better. You'll be amazed by the culinary dishes and excellent wine served in the warm interior of this gastropub. No fixed menu here, but a choice of two- to seven-course Chef's menu for lunch and dinner.

LINDENGRACHT 90, DAALDERAMSTERDAM.NL, 020-6248864, TRAM: 3 – NIEUWE WILLEMSSTRAAT

31 CAFÉ RESTAURANT AMSTERDAM

For classic bistro dishes that you can never go wrong with, there's Café Restaurant Amsterdam near the Westerpark. A modern brasserie in an old industrial water pumping station. The seafood platter here is recommended! Also perfect for larger groups or for taking the kids out to dinner.

WATERTORENPLEIN 6, CAFERESTAURANTAMSTERDAM.NL, 020-6822666, TRAM: 10 – VAN HALLSTRAAT

Bar Boca's

10 BAR BOCA'S

Shared dining is also a popular dining concept in Amsterdam, and they know all about this at Bar Boca's on the Westerstraat. You can order small sandwiches (Bocas) during the day, and meat, fish or veggie platters full of goodies to share with the whole table in the evening. Perfect with wine or a cold beer.

WESTERSTRAAT 30, BAR-BOCAS.NL, 020-8203727, TRAM: 3 & 10 – MARNIXPLEIN

13 TOSCANINI

Restaurant Toscanini has made a name for itself in Amsterdam. Authentic Italian food that always goes down well over six courses. The decor is just as simple and authentic, with a large open kitchen where you can see the chefs at work. A must for those who love that Italian atmosphere. But book well in advance to be sure of a table.

LINDENGRACHT 75, RESTAURANTTOSCANINI.NL, 020-6232813, TRAM: 3 – NIEUWE WILLEMSSTRAAT, TRAM: 10 – NASSAUKADE

2 SALMUERA

Salmuera is a neo-Argentinian restaurant on the Rozengracht. This hotspot serves bar bites, great cocktails and grilled meats. But they've also got a ceviche bar! Reserve an outdoor table, especially in the summer, because they have a wonderful and super romantic courtyard.

ROZENGRACHT 106, SAL-AMSTERDAM.NL, 020-6245752, TRAM: 13, 14 & 17 – MARNIXSTRAAT/ ROZENGRACHT

Salmuera

30 KOFFIE ENDE KOECK

Koffie ende Koeck is a nice vegan hotspot opposite the Westerpark, a cute little thing for coffee and healthy treats. Koffie ende Koeck is famous for its cinnamon rolls, which you definitely must try.

HAARLEMMERWEG 175,
KOFFIE-ENDEKOECK.NL, 020-7372731,
TRAM: 10 – VAN HALLSTRAAT

TIP!
Stroll through the narrow streets in the Jordaan and discover even more nice spots.

37 CAFÉ DE WALVIS

Café De Walvis was one of the first hotspots to open in the Spaarndammerbuurt. A cool café with lots of craft beers on the list and street art on the walls. Nice place for lunch or coffee during the day, and a popular spot for drinks in the evening. Great terrace for people-watching when the weather's good.

SPAARNDAMMERSTRAAT 516,
WALVIS-AMSTERDAM.NL, 020-7739374,
TRAM: 3 – HAARLEMMERPLEIN

27 TOKI

If you're looking for a hip coffee bar in the Jordaan, go to Toki. It's a cool hangout with a noteworthy interior. Think light and white, natural materials (wood and stone) and some nice graphics. They serve good coffee here, made with beans from the Berlin-based micro-roaster Bonanza Coffee Heroes.

BINNEN DOMMERSSTRAAT 15,
TOKIHO.AMSTERDAM, 020-3636009,
TRAM: 3 – HAARLEMMERPLEIN

1 BALTHAZAR'S KEUKEN

A living-room restaurant that gives you the feeling of sitting around a table with friends. The chef offers a three-course menu with surprising combinations every week. Choose a platter with five small starters to share, followed by a choice of fish or meat and a dessert.

ELANDSGRACHT 108, BALTHAZARS
KEUKEN.NL, TRAM: 7 & 10 – ELANDSGRACHT

Toki

JORDAAN

Mossel & Gin

32 MOSSEL & GIN

Mossel & Gin bar-restaurant is a jewel in the Westerpark. The name gives the game away, of course: they specialize in the preparation of mussels and gin and tonics. They have an enviable patio for summertime, illuminated by lights on long cords. An idyllic spot in the city centre.

GOSSCHALKLAAN 12, MOSSELENGIN.NL, 020-4865869, TRAM: 10 – VAN HALLSTRAAT

6 L'INVITÉ

This French restaurant tucked between houses in the heart of the Jordaan is a real hidden gem. They prepare French classics with an original twist here, and with only high quality meats and fish, and organic vegetables. L'Invité is also a perfect place for a romantic dinner.

BLOEMGRACHT 47, LINVITE.NL, 020-5702010, TRAM: 13, 14 & 17 – WESTERMARKT

G's

15 G'S

New York's brunch culture has finally reached Amsterdam, and one of the spots you should visit on Sunday is G's in the Jordaan. Typical brunch fare is served in a former pole-dancing club. Must try: a boozy brunch. G's serves the best Bloody Marys.

GOUDSBLOEMSTRAAT 9, REALLYNICEPLACE.COM, TRAM: 3 – NIEUWE WILLEMSSTRAAT, TRAM: 10 – NASSAUKADE

8 GIN NEO BISTRO & WINES

Gin Neo Bistro & Wines on the corner of the Westerstraat and Marnixstraat is a new-style bistro, inspired by Parisian bistros but with an industrial touch. The dishes look beautiful and taste as good as they look. They serve a changing menu of five, six or seven courses every month, prepared with seasonal ingredients.

WESTERSTRAAT 264, GINAMSTERDAM.COM, 020-6279932, TRAM: 3 & 10 – MARNIXPLEIN

36 BOCCONI

Bocconi is a cosy Italian eatery in the Spaarndammerbuurt, within walking distance of Bar Mick, Café De Walvis and DopHert. Nowhere will you find as many different bruschettas on the menu as at this neighbourhood restaurant. But Bocconi is particularly popular for its gluten-free pasta dishes!

SPAARNDAMMERSTRAAT 17, BOCCONISANI.NL, 020-2336407, TRAM: 3 – HAARLEMMERPLEIN

38 DOPHERT

You find more and more vegan spots in Amsterdam, DopHert being one of them. A hip lunchroom on the Spaarndammerstraat that also does takeaways. They also organise a healthy vegan dinner every first Thursday of the month, which is a must for learning that vegan food is anything but bland.

SPAARNDAMMERSTRAAT 49, DOPHERTCATERING.NL, 020-7520581, TRAM: 3 – HAARLEMMERPLEIN

TIP!
More and more nice hotspots are opening along the up-and-coming Spaarndammer-straat behind the Westerpark.

39 BAR MICK

In this part of West, Spaarn-dammerstraat is undoubtedly where it all happens. You're welcome all day at Bar Mick, from breakfast to lunch and from coffee to dinner and drinks. A typical all-day hotspot with a no-nonsense atmosphere and a small menu with simple but good food.

SPAARNDAMMERSTRAAT 53, BARMICK.NL, 020-3702273, TRAM: 3 – HAARLEMMERPLEIN

JORDAAN

Gin Neo Bistro & Wines

137

SHOPPING

TIP!
The Haarlem-
merstraat and
Haarlemmerdijk
are the Jordaan's
not-to-be-
missed streets.

4 SNEAKER DISTRICT

Sneaker District is without doubt
the coolest place for sneakers in
Amsterdam. You'll find the must-
have sneakers of the season at this
store on the Rozengracht.

ROZENGRACHT 21, SNEAKERDISTRICT.NL,
020-7894962, TRAM: 13, 14 & 17 –
MARNIXSTRAAT/ROZENGRACHT

7 ROBINS HOOD

The concept store Robins Hood
is tucked away in the Jordaan's
narrow streets. You can get fair
trade urban accessories with a
story here. The artisanal products
are all one of a kind, and mostly
locally produced, so Amsterdam
through and through. Their
collection of fair-trade shawls and
bags will render you greedy.

TWEEDE TUINDWARSSTRAAT 7,
ROBINSHOOD.NL, 020-3637486, TRAM: 3 &
10 – MARNIXPLEIN

18 MY-OH-MY

MY-OH MY began by setting
up shop at festivals. This was so
successful that an online shop,
pop-up store and permanent store
soon followed. They sell a well-
curated mix of new clothes and
customized vintage, accessories
and handcrafted jewellery. Trendy
clothes at affordable prices.

HAARLEMMERSTRAAT 85, MYOHMY.NL,
020-3639657, TRAM: 1, 2, 5, 13 & 17 –
CENTRAAL STATION WESTZIJDE

Store without a home

Robins Hood

3 LES DEUX FRÈRES
Sad news for the ladies, but Les Deux Frères only sells fashion for men. Two brothers opened this shop with the purpose of dressing men from head to toe. This is where Dutch sobriety meets French flair. Besides clothing, they also sell accessories, such as sunglasses, bags and jewellery.

ROZENGRACHT 58, LESDEUXFRERES.NL, 020-8464613, TRAM: 13, 14 & 17 – MARNIXSTRAAT/ ROZENGRACHT

22 STORE WITHOUT A HOME
You can find inspiration for your home at Store Without a Home. In addition to furniture, this interior design store also sells very nice accessories by designers and brands that are not yet big names or mainstream. Nothing mass-produced, only unique items ready to add a personal touch to your home. A mecca for shopping for beautiful gifts, too.

HAARLEMMERDIJK 26, STOREWITHOUTAHOME.NL, TRAM: 3 – HAARLEMMERPLEIN

25 RESTORED
You'll find a very special collection of jewellery, clothing, home accessories and books at Restored on the Haarlemmerdijk. The items are mostly handmade, and the designs one of a kind. You can find whatever's hip in cities like New York and Paris at this little concept store.

HAARLEMMERDIJK 39, RESTORED.NL, 020-3376473, TRAM: 3 – HAARLEMMERPLEIN

Sukha

9 INDIANAWEG10

Real gems are often hidden in the Jordaan. The mini department store Indianaweg10 is tucked away on the Tichelstraat, and was set up by two sisters with a love for treasure hunting. You'll find a collection based on the eternal search for the most beautiful stuff, from organic beauty products to furniture, vintage clothing and accessories.

TICHELSTRAAT 12, INDIANAWEG10.COM, TRAM: 10 – MARNIXPLEIN

TIP!
Keep your eyes open for the most striking street art in the Jordaan.

21 SUKHA

You can't be blamed for falling in love with Sukha on the Haarlemmerstraat, an eco-friendly mini department store where you'll find Dutch design and handcrafted items from India and Nepal, made from pure, natural materials. They sell clothes, bags, jewellery and furniture in predominantly natural tones.

HAARLEMMERSTRAAT 110, SUKHA-AMSTERDAM.NL, 020-3304001, TRAM: 1, 2, 5, 13 & 17 – CENTRAAL STATION

26 MARBLES VINTAGE

There's no shortage of vintage shops in the Haarlemmerbuurt. If you like nosing through racks for that one important find, then Marbles Vintage is the place for you. This vintage department store has two floors and sells a mix of sixties to nineties clothing, accessories, shoes and bags. At very affordable prices, too. Tip: Marbles also has branches on the Ferdinand Bolstraat and the Staalstraat.

HAARLEMMERDIJK 64, 020-7508146, TRAM: 3 – HAARLEMMERPLEIN

Indianaweg10

JORDAAN

28 CONCRETE MATTER

Looking for the perfect gift for a
man? Then the gift shop Concrete
Matter is your answer: they sell
only items for men. You feel
like a real world traveller here,
surrounded by globes, antique
furniture and vintage items from
around the world, and you'll find
everything for the stylish man.

HAARLEMMERDIJK 127, CONCRETE-
MATTER.COM, 020-2610933,
TRAM: 3 – HAARLEMMERPLEIN

24 THIS IS HAPPENING

Need a style upgrade? You can
get a haircut *and* shop at the
salon/shop This is happening.
They sell beautiful fashion labels,
accessories and cool gadgets
inspired by street trends in the

TIP!
Nowhere in
Amsterdam will
you find as many
concept stores
for men as in
the Haarlem-
merbuurt on
the edge of the
Jordaan.

world's big cities. Walk in for an
extended hair session or simply
to take a look at the crave-worthy
toys on offer.

HAARLEMMERDIJK 40,
THIS-IS-HAPPENING.NL, 020-6202440,
TRAM: 3 – HAARLEMMERPLEIN

20 IBERICUS

If you like Spanish delicatessen,
then stroll over to specialist store
Ibericus, opposite Sukha and
Vinnies. The only meat products
sold at this unique store are from
the Iberian pig. You can buy ham
to enjoy with drinks at home or
for a picnic in the park, but it's
probably more fun to have a plate
with a glass of wine right there at
the back of the deli.

HAARLEMMERSTRAAT 93,
FACEBOOK.COM/IBERICUSAMSTERDAM,
020-2236573, TRAM: 1, 2, 5, 13 & 17 –
CENTRAAL STATION WESTZIJDE

29 DIS

Don't feel like cooking?
Then traiteur Dis on the
Haarlemmerplein is the answer!
You get a choice of seasonal dishes
that are simple and healthy. Also
nice: if you don't eat carbs, you
get the same dish for the same
price but with extra vegetables
or a salad. If you're visiting

Concrete Matter

Tenue de Nîmes

Amsterdam, this is where to get what you need for a picnic in the Westerpark.

HAARLEMMERPLEIN 37, EATDIS.NL, TRAM: 3 –
HAARLEMMERPLEIN

23 SIX AND SONS

You will find a surprising number of stores in the Jordaan that focus only on men. Six and Sons used to be one such store. The good news: they now also sell a cool women's collection. This concept store also sells an extraordinary collection of vintage items, from old maps to whiskey glasses.

HAARLEMMERDIJK 31, SIXANDSONS.COM,
020-2330092, TRAM: 3 – HAARLEMMERPLEIN

19 TENUE DE NÎMES

You'll find the finest fashion labels at Tenue de Nîmes, a concept store that has made a name for itself in Amsterdam. They've got branches on both the Elandsgracht and the Haarlemmerstraat. A shopper's paradise for men, although the store on the Haarlemmerstraat also carries a good collection for woman. Their main focus is on denim and other cool items. Have a Lot Sixty One coffee while you shop.

- ELANDSGRACHT 60, TENUEDENIMES.COM,
  020-3204012, TRAM: 7 & 10 – ELANDSGRACHT
- HAARLEMMERSTRAAT 92, TENUEDENIMES.COM,
  020-3312778, TRAM: 1, 2, 5, 13 & 17 – CENTRAAL
  STATION WESTZIJDE

MY LITTLE BLACK BOOK

THE CANAL
DISTRICT
& 9 STREETS

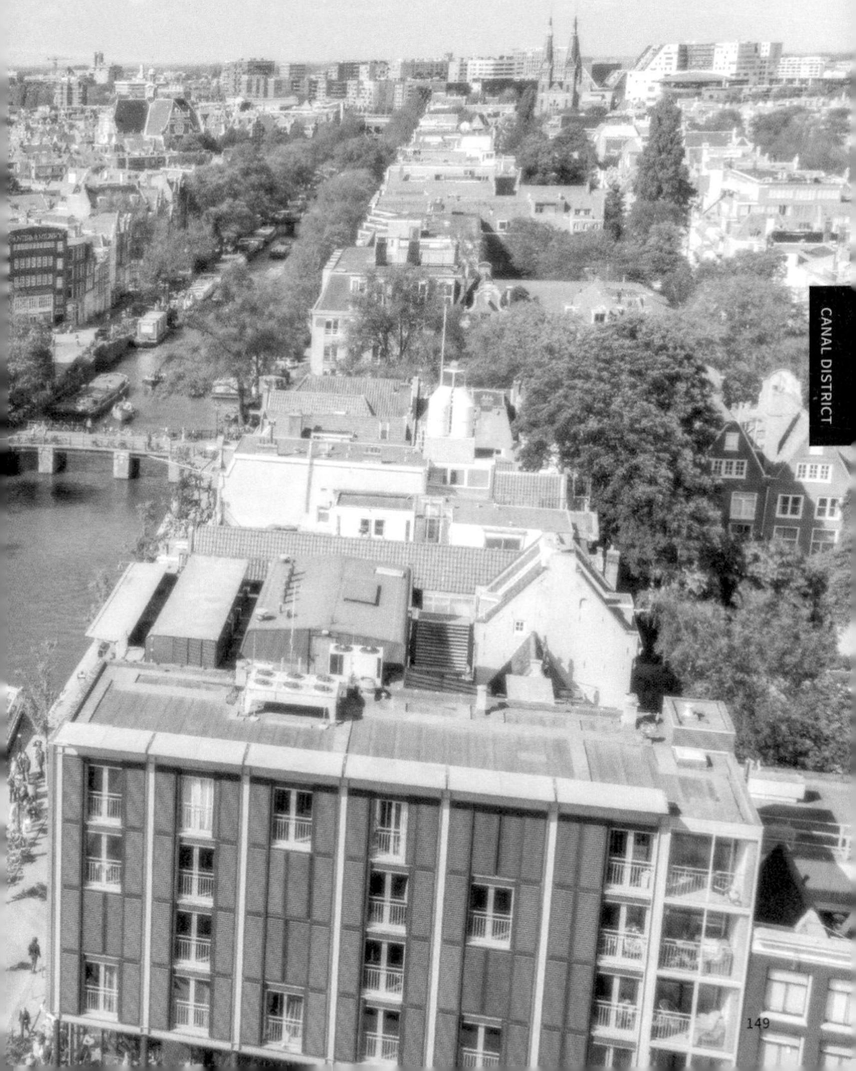

Amsterdam is known for its beautiful Canal District, stretching from the Amstel to the Haarlemmerstraat and from the Singel to the Prinsengracht. The nicest spots are hidden between the stately historic buildings on the canals and the side streets. Stroll along the canals and discover the Nine Streets and the Utrechtsestraat, shop at small boutiques and have a drink at one of the cosy cafés.

BUCKET LIST

12 Museum of Bags and Purses

Fashionistas couldn't be happier at the Museum of Bags and Purses, in a beautiful 17th-century building on the Herengracht. With more than 5,000 bags in its permanent collection, this is the largest bag museum in the world. Combine your visit with an extended high tea in one of the period rooms.

HERENGRACHT 573, TASSENMUSEUM.NL, 020-5246452, TRAM: 4, 9 & 14 – REMBRANDTPLEIN

14 Tuschinski

Pathé Tuschinski is the most beautiful cinema you'll find in Amsterdam. This was originally a theatre, and you can see this reflected in the entrance and main auditorium: the beautiful red carpet, art deco and art nouveau elements, balconies and loveseats in Auditorium 1. Perfect for a date night!

REGULIERSBREESTRAAT 26-34, PATHE.NL, 0900-2357284, TRAM: 4, 9, 14, 16 & 24 – MUNTPLEIN

17 The Nine Streets

Without doubt the cosiest nine streets in the Canal District. Discover the Gasthuismolensteeg, Oude Spiegelstraat, Wijde Heisteeg, Wolvenstraat, Hartenstraat, Huidenstraat, Reestraat, Runstraat and the Berenstraat. These together are Amsterdam's Nine Streets, and *the* place to shop, with nice concept stores and fashion boutiques. Make sure you check out the Hazenstraat as well, which people refer to as the tenth street.

8 Foam

Photography fans must be sure to visit Foam. With its changing exhibitions, this is where to see the work of world-renowned photographers *and* that of emerging talent. Check the website beforehand to see what's on!

KEIZERSGRACHT 609, FOAM.ORG, 020-5516500, TRAM: 16 & 24 – KEIZERSGRACHT/VIJZELSTRAAT

4 Utrechtsestraat

The Utrechtsestraat is known as one of the nicest shopping streets in Amsterdam. Stretching from the Rembrandtplein to the Frederiksplein, it is lined with beautiful fashion and concept stores, coffee bars and restaurants. A perfect street for shopping if you're looking for something special and want to avoid the busy shopping streets.

CANAL DISTRICT

THE CANAL
DISTRICT
& 9 STREETS

TOUR 5

1. BOCCA
2. LAVINIA GOOD FOOD
3. BUFFET VAN ODETTE
4. UTRECHTSESTRAAT
5. BAR MOUSTACHE
6. MAISONNL
7. TEMPO DOELOE
8. FOAM
9. GEITENWOLLEN-WINKEL
10. KIBOOTS
11. LITE/DARK
12. MUSEUM OF BAGS AND PURSES
13. GUTS & GLORY
14. TUSCHINSKI
15. THE FRENCH CONNECTION
16. HOPPA!
17. THE NINE STREETS
18. MARIE STELLA MARIS
19. THE DARLING
20. VENUS & ADONIS
21. EPISODE
22. WOLVENSTRAAT 23
23. KO GOLD
24. LAURA DOLS
25. MAISON RIKA
26. RIKA BOUTIQUE
27. LOTTI'S
28. FABIENNE CHAPOT
29. REE7
30. ZOË KARSSEN
31. OU.
32. PLUK
33. THE PELICAN STUDIO
34. WE ARE LABELS
35. RESTAURANT BREDA
36. DE LUWTE
37. CAFÉ DE KLEPEL
38. JD WILLIAM'S WHISKY BAR
39. PROPERTY OF…
40. TALES & SPIRITS
41. LOUIS

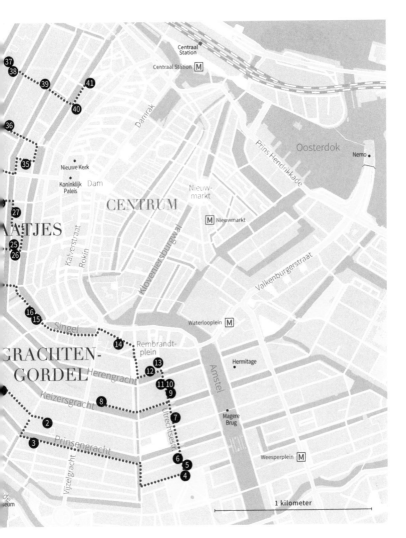

Centraal Station

Centraal Station Ⓜ

Damrak

Oosterdok

Nemo

Prins Hendrikkade

Nieuwe Kerk

Koninklijk Paleis

Dam

CENTRUM

Nieuw-markt

Ⓜ Nieuwmarkt

AATJES

Kalverstraat

Rokin

Kloveniersburgwal

Valkenburgerstraat

Waterlooplein Ⓜ

Singel

Rembrandt-plein

Hermitage

GRACHTEN-GORDEL

Herengracht

Amstel

Keizersgracht

Utrechtsestr.

Prinsengracht

Magere Brug

Weesperplein Ⓜ

Vijzelgracht

seum

1 kilometer

FOOD& DRINK

5 BAR MOUSTACHE

Bar Moustache on the Utrechtsestraat is the sort of place where you feel at home all day. A nice spot for coffee, lunch, dinner or a drink. The menu lists Italian dishes, and the atmosphere is always nice. In summertime, make sure you score a spot by the window so you can sit on the sill with the window open.

UTRECHTSESTRAAT 141,
BARMOUSTACHE.NL, 020-4281074,
TRAM: 4 – FREDERIKSPLEIN

TIP!
De Luwte is my secret spot for romantic dinners with my lover.

36 DE LUWTE

There is no restaurant as warm and cosy as De Luwte. This hidden gem is a must if you're planning a romantic dinner with your partner. Start the evening with a cocktail, then let yourself be amazed by the delicious French-Mediterranean cuisine. You definitely must try the tomahawk steak, a classic. Tip: Book a table by the window, overlooking the canal!

LELIEGRACHT 26,
RESTAURANTDELUWTE.NL, 020-6258548,
TRAM: 13, 14 & 17 – WESTERMARKT

20 VENUS & ADONIS

The steak restaurant Venus & Adonis is located halfway along the Prinsengracht. A beautiful, classically styled spot with a modern touch. Think tiled floors, dark wood and green velvet chairs, a place to fall in love with immediately. The terrace is a lovely place to sit in the summer. What to order? A surf and turf!

PRINSENGRACHT 274,
VENUSENADONIS.NL, 020-4211848,
TRAM: 13, 14 & 17 – WESTERMARKT

De Luwte

The French Connection

38 JD WILLIAM'S WHISKY BAR

You'll find the J.D. William's Whisky Bar between the Prinsengracht and Keizersgracht. With a chesterfield sofa, wooden tables and wrought iron chairs, this whisky bar is everything a whisky bar should be: dark and warm. It's got a surprising menu featuring pan-Asian cuisine. Not a pure whisky fan? Then try the whisky cocktails!

PRINSENSTRAAT 5, JDWILLIAMSWHISKYBAR.COM, 020-3620663, TRAM: 13, 14 & 17 – WESTERMARKT

15 THE FRENCH CONNECTION

You can find French cuisine in several areas in Amsterdam, including the Canal District. The French Connection is in the basement of the old Odeon building on the Singel. A beautifully decorated spot with a rural industrial interior and a menu of fine French dishes. All dishes are medium sized, so these 'tapas a la Francaise' are perfect for sharing.

SINGEL 460, TFCRESTAURANT.NL, 020-7373051, TRAM: 1, 2 & 5 – KONINGSPLEIN

7 TEMPO DOELOE

If there's one place in Amsterdam where you can get delicious Indonesian food, it's Tempo Doeloe. Not a hotspot, but it serves really tasty and affordable food. So end your day of shopping on the Utrechtsestraat with a meal at this authentic restaurant awarded with a Bib Gourmand from Michelin.

UTRECHTSESTRAAT 75, TEMPODOELOERESTAURANT.NL, 020-6257618, TRAM: 4 – KEIZERSGRACHT

Guts & Glory

13 GUTS & GLORY

There's a very special restaurant just around the corner from the Museum of Bags and Purses: Guts & Glory. Every six months a different animal takes centre stage on the menu, inspiring the creation of pure dishes prepared according to the "nose to tail" principle. All you have to do is decide on the number of courses: four, five, six or seven.

UTRECHTSESTRAAT 6, GUTSGLORY.NL, 020-3620030, TRAM: 4, 9 & 14 – REMBRANDTPLEIN

3 BUFFET VAN ODETTE

Good spots don't always have to be new and hip. Buffet van Odette is the sort of classic spot you keep coming back to. This bistro-style restaurant in a beautiful corner building on the Prinsengracht is renowned for its good price-quality balance, and is open from lunch to dinnertime.

PRINSENGRACHT 598, BUFFET-AMSTERDAM.NL, 020-4236034, TRAM: 7 & 10 – SPIEGELGRACHT

37 CAFÉ DE KLEPEL

The Prinsenstraat boasts one of the best gastropubs in Amsterdam. Café De Klepel may look like a pub, but its food far transcends anything you find at your average pub. It operates on the table d'hote concept, with a season-based daily-changing three- or four-course menu. If you'd like to enjoy an extended dinner here, then we suggest you reserve a table.

PRINSENSTRAAT 22, CAFEDEKLEPEL.NL, TRAM: 3 & 10 – MARNIXPLEIN

Café De Klepel

YOURLITTLEBLACKBOOK.ME

32 PLUK

Step inside Pluk and you won't
want to leave. This hotspot has
a fresh white décor, wooden
parquet floors and a beautiful
marble counter. You'll find crates
of fresh fruit from which they
make the most delicious juices,
finger-licking cakes, herb plants
on the windowsills and a menu
packed with healthy organic
breakfast and lunch dishes. While
your breakfast or lunch is being
prepared, you can shop shop for
the nicest home items or for an
original gift for a friend.
REESTRAAT 19, PLUK9STRAATJES.NL,
020-3301254, TRAM: 13, 14 & 15 –
WESTERMARKT

TIP!
Whenever I go
shopping on the
Nine Streets,
I always have
something to
eat and drink at
hotspots Ree7
or Pluk.

29 REE7

Everything is homemade at this
cosy restaurant on the Reestraat.
Ree7 opens for breakfast at 9 in
the morning and serves lunch
all-day long. On the menu
you find dishes like pancakes,
sandwiches, salads and soups.
The décor: wooden tables, cool
lamps, colourful pillows, fresh
flowers on the bar and cheerful
pompoms hanging from tall twigs
in flowerpots. Be warned: the
atmosphere is so cosy and homely
that you won't want to leave.
REESTRAAT 7, REE7.NL, 020-3301254,
TRAM: 13, 14 & 15 – WESTERMARKT

2 LAVINIA GOOD FOOD

If you didn't know that a beautiful
hotspot like Lavinia Good Food
existed on the Kerkstraat, you'd
probably walk right past this
street. Everything here revolves
around healthy and organic food,
prepared with local ingredients
and containing no unnecessary
additives. The interior is homey
and warm, and it is always busy.
They serve coffee from Bocca,
which is located just down the
street!
KERKSTRAAT 176, LAVINIAGOODFOOD.
NL, 020-6261432, TRAM: 16 & 24 –
KEIZERSGRACHT

Ree7

Pluk

1 BOCCA

Amsterdam coffee-roasters Bocca have created a real coffee mecca on the Kerkstraat: a training centre, roastery, shop and coffee bar in one. Learn all about the latest coffee techniques or take a seat at the bar and and observe the male baristas preparing the best coffee.

KERKSTRAAT 96, BOCCA.NL, TRAM: 1, 2 & 5 – PRINSENGRACHT

40 TALES & SPIRITS

Tales & Spirits cocktail bar is tucked away in a narrow alley between the Singel and the Spui. You can drink awesome cocktails here with special ingredients. What you might not expect is that they also offer very tasty food, small dishes that are perfect for sharing, and for which they'd be more than happy to recommend a cocktail pairing.

LIJNBAANSSTEEG 5-7, TALESANDSPIRITS.COM, TRAM: 1, 2, 5, 13 & 17 – NIEUWEZIJDSE KOLK

27 LOTTI'S

Few hotel lobbies are as atmospheric as The Hoxton's café-restaurant Lotti's in Amsterdam. It's a lovely spot for coffee or a cocktail, lunch or something to eat in the evening. The interior is cool and colourful, like sitting in a fancy joint in Brooklyn, New York. Sink into one of the velvet sofas as you sip your cocktail or coffee after shopping on the Nine Streets.

HERENGRACHT 255, LOTTIS.COM, 020-8885555, TRAM: 13 & 17 – DAM/RAADHUISSTRAAT

Lotti's

Hoppa!

16 HOPPA!

HOPPA! is a nice spot in the centre for beer lovers. They serve beer from Amsterdam microbreweries at this small pub in the stately Odeon building on the Singel (which once housed a brewery itself). They offer thirty locally brewed craft beers, served from tap or bottle.

SINGEL 460, HOPPA.AMSTERDAM, 020-3446432, TRAM: 1, 2 & 5 – KONINGSPLEIN

35 RESTAURANT BREDA

This restaurant takes its name from its owner's city of origin. You can experience that city's jovial and Burgundian atmosphere at this spot in Amsterdam. Restaurant Breda's menu changes every day. All *you* need to decide is whether to have meat, fish or vegetarian, or whether to go for the basic, medium or full-monty menu, each of which consists of five courses.

SINGEL 210, BREDA-AMSTERDAM.COM, 020-6225233, TRAM: 13 & 17 – DAM/RAADHUISSTRAAT

22 WOLVENSTRAAT 23

Amsterdammers also refer to this spot on the Wolvenstraat 23 as "The Wolfie". It's a popular café in the Nine Streets, and whether this is down to the laidback cosiness, the delicious Asian snacks, the good music or the cocktails, Wolfies has simply been a great spot for years!

WOLVENSTRAAT 23, FACEBOOK.COM/ WOLVENSTRAAT-23-1451239075117871, 020-3200843, TRAM: 1, 2 & 5 – SPUI/NIEUWEZIJDS VOORBURGWAL

41 LOUIS

Where would Amsterdam be without a good pub at which the taps flow freely and you can nibble classic bar snacks. A brown café with a cool twist in the form of industrial elements, the wooden floor and exposed brick wall. Louis on the Singel is such a café. Don't be surprised if a ginger cat climbs unto your lap without warning.

SINGEL 43, LOUIS-AMSTERDAM.NL, 020-7526328, TRAM: 1, 2, 5, 13 & 17 – NIEUWEZIJDS KOLK

TIP!
The Hoxton's lobby is one of my favourite places to meet up with friends at the weekend.

11 LITE/DARK

Parched from all that shopping on the Utrechtsestraat? Then go get a juice or smoothie at LITE/DARK. You'll find only healthy things for an energy boost here. Find a spot on the sofa, or in the window frame to people-watch.

UTRECHTSESTRAAT 22, LITEDARK.NL, 020-7539919, TRAM: 4 – KEIZERSGRACHT

CANAL DISTRICT

Louis

SHOPPING

31 OU.

OU. is on the same street as Pluk and Ree7. This boutique is a mini department store selling clothes, shoes and home accessories. Within OU.'s walls you'll also find a concession of The City Street Spa! So, shop *and* relax.

REESTRAAT 16, OU-AMSTERDAM.COM, 020-4202186, TRAM: 13, 14 & 17 – WESTERMARKT

TIP!
Zigzag along the Nine Streets to avoid missing anything in this shopper's paradise.

18 MARIE STELLA MARIS

Marie Stella Maris is a Dutch lifestyle brand that sells natural body care products and mineral water. The packaging alone is a thing of beauty. The café in the basement is also quite special! The entrance on the Keizersgracht is barely noticeable, but settle down here for a coffee, breakfast with a croissant, or a glass of water.

KEIZERSGRACHT 357, MARIE-STELLA-MARIS.COM, 085-2732845, TRAM: 1, 2 & 5 – SPUI/NIEUWEZIJDS VOORBURGWAL

30 ZOË KARSSEN

The Amsterdam brand Zoe Karssen is famous for its easy-to-wear items with controversial prints and slogans. The clothes have a rock 'n' roll edge and are beloved by celebrities all over the world. You'll find its entire collection of clothing and perfumes at this flagship store in Amsterdam.

REESTRAAT 9, ZOEKARSSEN.COM, 020-7797771, TRAM: 13, 14 & 17 – WESTERMARKT

Marie Stella Maris

Fabienne Chapot

28 FABIENNE CHAPOT

The quintessentially Dutch brand Fabienne Chapot is on the Hartenstraat in the Nine Streets. It began with beautiful leather bags, shoes and accessories such as wallets and key chains, but now also sells clothes and shawls. You can score good leather basics here, or that one colourful bang on-trend eye-catcher.

HARTENSTRAAT 7, FAB.NL, 020-4226683, TRAM: 1, 2 & 5 – DAM/PALEISSTRAAT

10 KIBOOTS

Kiboots on the Utrechtsestraat is known for its brown leather boots made from vintage kilim carpets with colourful oriental prints. But they sell much more than boots. You can also buy beautiful jewellery, clothes and home accessories. This store is a must for anyone who loves the bohemian style.

UTRECHTSESTRAAT 47, KIBOOTS.NL, 020-7722942, TRAM: 4 – KEIZERSGRACHT

21 EPISODE

You'll find the vintage shop Episode just a few doors down from Wolvenstraat 23. It's one of the biggest vintage and second-hand clothes shops in Amsterdam, with several branches. All the clothes are carefully selected and in line with the latest fashion trends in the glossies. Hunt through the racks and discover unique items that no one else owns.

BERENSTRAAT 1, EPISODE.EU, 020-6264679, TRAM: 1, 2 & 5 – SPUI/NIEUWEZIJDS VOORBURGWAL

The Darling

19 THE DARLING

At The Darling you'll find a mix of new and vintage accessories, clothes and stuff for the home. It's like stepping into a living room, where everything happens to be for sale. Order a cup of tea or coffee with something sweet to nibble and calmly take everything in. You can also buy items from the store's own label, customised thus unique!

RUNSTRAAT 4, THEDARLINGAMSTERDAM.NL, 020-4223142, TRAM: 1, 2 & 5 – SPUI/ NIEUWEZIJDS VOORBURGWAL

25-26 RIKA

Rika's distinctive bags with the star motif have been a fashion statement since the launch. The label was founed by fashion polymath Ulrika Lundgren, and you step into the world of Rika the moment you walk through the door. The bags, clothes and accessories are both timeless and amazing. Maison Rika, the more lifestyle-oriented Rika shop, is on the corner of the Spiegelstraat, and also offers lodging in its exclusive suite.

MAISON RIKA, OUDE SPIEGELSTRAAT 12 & RIKA BOUTIQUE, OUDE SPIEGELSTRAAT 9, RIKASTUDIOS.COM, 020-3301112 TRAM: 1, 2 & 5 – SPUI/NIEUWEZIJDS VOORBURGWAL

TIP!
We Are Labels has branches all over the city and is my favourite place for affordable trendy clothes.

34 WE ARE LABELS

Update your wardrobe at We Are Labels! You'll find branches of this fashion label at various locations across the city, including the Utrechtsestraat (no. 68 for women, no. 36 for men). But their most beautiful branch is surely the 400m² concept store on the Raadhuisstraat, in which you'll also find a concession store of the wonderful Swedish beauty brand L:A Bruket.

UTRECHTSESTRAAT 68/36, RAADHUIS-STRAAT 46-50, WEARELABELS.COM, 020-3313850, TRAM: 4 – PRINSENGRACHT

CANAL DISTRICT

L:A BRUKET

We Are Labels

6 MAISONNL

Some stores surprise you with every visit. MaisonNL achieves this through its frequently changing collection of home accessories, jewellery and clothing for women and kids. Their collection consists of carefully selected special items that also make perfect original gifts.

UTRECHTSESTRAAT 118, MAISONNL.COM, 020-4285183, TRAM: 4 – PRINSENGRACHT

TIP!
For boutique shopping, go to the Canal District and the Nine Streets.

23 KO GOLD

There are stores you walk into with nothing specific in mind and leave with a wish list as long as your arm. You can score some fun things at the concept store Ko Gold on the Wolvenstraat, from laptop sleeves to cookbooks, jewellery to items for the home.

WOLVENSTRAAT 8, 020-7372102, TRAM: 4 – KEIZERSGRACHT

24 LAURA DOLS

Vintage fan? Then you've got to visit Laura Dols. What distinguishes this particular vintage store from others is its collection of fifties clothing. And you're especially likely to strike gold if you're after glitz and glamour. Planning a wedding? Ask to see their huge collection of vintage wedding dresses.

WOLVENSTRAAT 7, LAURADOLS.NL, 020-6249066, TRAM: 1, 2 & 5 – SPUI/ NIEUWEZIJDS VOORBURGWAL

Laura Dols

Geitenwollenwinkel

9 GEITENWOLLENWINKEL

Sustainable shopping isn't boring when done at the Geitenwollenwinkel! All the clothes here are "green, honest and vegan". Fine, soft basic items from natural materials that are good for you *and* the environment.

UTRECHTSESTRAAT 37, GEITENWOLLENWINKEL.NL, 020-3620784, TRAM: 4 – KEIZERSGRACHT

39 PROPERTY OF…

Property Of … is a must-not-miss shop for stylish men. They sell everything for the urban lifestyle here: very fine bags and accessories made from high-quality materials, with a personal touch in the form of name engraving. It's like walking into 1920s bar full of stylish items for gents.

HERENSTRAAT 2, THEPROPERTYOF.COM, 020-6225909, TRAM: 13, 14 & 17 – WESTERMARKT

33 THE PELICAN STUDIO

Somewhat hidden, this store, but definitely recommended. A concept store that could give its equivalents in New York or Paris a run for their money. They carry several truly beautiful brands, including Scandinavian labels, for him, her and the kids, and you can also have a coffee in the Pelican Café.

RAADHUISSTRAAT 35, THEPELICANSTUDIO.COM, 020-3638024, TRAM: 13, 14 & 17 – WESTERMARKT

MY LITTLE BLACK BOOK

NORTH

NDSM Wharf

You're in North in no time by ferry. This is undoubtedly the most rugged district in Amsterdam. Lots of the old factories and warehouses here have been converted into trendy restaurants. In summertime, NDSM Wharf is the place for festivals. You get a great view of the city's skyline from Amsterdam North.

BUCKET LIST

1 Go North by ferry

It feels wonderful to get some fresh air while out on the water, and it really feels like you're leaving the city when you take the ferry to North from behind Central Station. For this reason especially, stand with your bike on the open deck and watch the rugged North come to you. Ferries go to NDSM Wharf and the Buiksloterweg.

29 EYE Film Museum

You cannot ignore the EYE building. It is above all a place you must visit if you love film. It hosts a changing series of exhibitions in the film museum, and screens cult movies in its cinema rooms. Tip: before your screening, grab a bite in the brasserie overlooking Amsterdam.

IJPROMENADE 1, EYEFILM.NL, 020-5891400, FERRY TO BUIKSLOTERWEG

32 LOOKOUT

From A'DAM Lookout on the roof of A'DAM Toren (Tower), you get a spectacular 360-degree view of Amsterdam, including the historic centre, the port and the polder landscape north of the city. You'll also find Europe's highest swing. Once fastened into the safety harness, you get to swing over the edge of the tower at the terrifying height of almost 100 meters above ground.

OVERHOEKSPLEIN 1, ADAMTOREN.NL, FERRY TO BUIKSLOTERWEG

4 NDSM Wharf

If you visit North, NDSM Wharf is not to be missed. It's an old shipyard with lots of warehouses and street art. Dozens of festivals take place here in the summer, and you'll also find a variety of restaurant hotspots here.

26 Tolhuistuin

The Tolhuistuin is a creative incubator occupying old Shell buildings on the bank of the IJ. Events are staged here in both winter and summer, and you can also attend concerts organised by the Paradiso club. The garden looks magical in the evening with its glowing lights.

TOLHUISWEG 5, TOLHUISTUIN.NL, FERRY TO BUIKSLOTERWEG

NORTH

TOUR 6

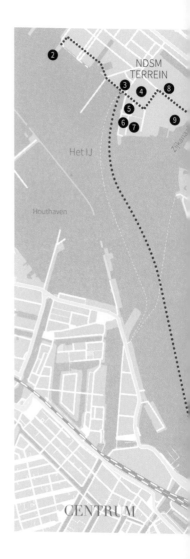

1. FERRY TO NORTH
2. LOETJE AAN HET IJ
3. PONTSTATION
4. NDSM WHARF
5. BISTRO NOORD
6. WOODIES AT BERLIN
7. PLLEK
8. IJ-HALLEN
9. NOORDERLICHT
10. NEEF LOUIS
11. VAN DIJK & KO
12. THE ROLLING ROCK KITCHEN
13. BLOM & BLOM
14. CAFÉ DE CEUVEL
15. DE SOEPBOER
16. SMAAQT
17. PEKMARKT
18. PEK & KLEREN
19. FASHION & TEA
20. CAFÉ MODERN
21. HANGAR
22. HOTEL DE GOUDFAZANT
23. STORK
24. OEDIPUS TAPROOM
25. IL PECORINO
26. TOLHUISTUIN
27. THT
28. THE COFFEE VIRUS
29. EYE FILM MUSEUM
30. MADAM
31. MOON
32. LOOKOUT

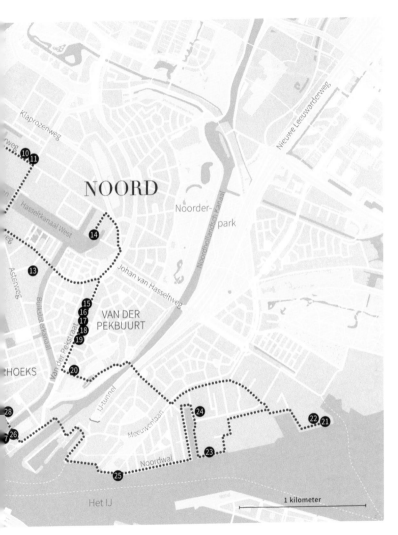

NORTH

FOOD& DRINK

TIP!
NDSM Wharf in summer is one of my favourite spots along the water.

7 PLLEK

Pllek is an especially popular spot in summer. A huge bar built from old shipping containers with – as the icing on the cake – a city beach on the banks of the IJ. This is where hip Amsterdam goes for a beer with delicious bar food. There's often live music here on Sundays.

TT. NEVERITAWEG 59, PLLEK.NL,
020-2900020, FERRY TO NDSM WHARF

9 NOORDERLICHT

Noorderlicht was one of the first eateries on the NDSM Wharf. It's a creative café that gives you the feeling of being miles from the city. When the weather's good, it's a great place to sprawl on the grass with a cold drink while you enjoy some live music. There are regular performances here, so check the schedule.

NDSM-PLEIN 102,
NOORDERLICHTCAFE.NL, 020-4922770,
FERRY TO NDSM WHARF

5 BISTRO NOORD

Bistro Noord is famous for its classic traditional dishes, but what makes this spot extra special is the combination of its industrial design and the warm vibe of a French bistro. It's the sort of place where you feel immediately at home and stay for an extended dinner. *The* place for a culinary evening on the NDSM Wharf.

MT. ONDINAWEG 32, BISTRONOORD.NL,
020-7059906, FERRY TO NDSM WHARF

Café Modern

Stork

20 CAFÉ MODERN

Café Modern is a restaurant with a story. This hotspot in the Van der Pekbuurt occupies an old building that used to be a bank, as you'll notice when you visit the toilets, which are, in fact, in the vault. The décor is vintage, and there's a different surprise on the menu every day as they go by the table d'hote concept.

MEIDOORNWEG 2, MODERNAMSTERDAM.NL, 020-4940684, BUS: 38 & 105 – MEIDOORNPLEIN

23 STORK

For seafood lovers, this is a not-to-be-missed restaurant on the North side of the IJ. We recommend the fruits de mer platter. Stork is located in an old industrial warehouse on the banks of the IJ, and it's lovely to sit here in summer looking out over the water and skyline.

GEDEMPT HAMERKANAAL 201, RESTAURANTSTORK.NL, 020-6344000, BUS: 38 & 105 – HAVIKSLAAN

25 IL PECORINO

In front of a wood-fired oven stands an Italian chef making the best pizzas in North, using nothing but pure Italian ingredients, which you taste with every bite. Il Pecorino is very nicely located, too: on the Wilhelminadok, thus right on the water.

NOORDWAL 1, ILPECORINO.NL, 020-7371511, BUS: 38 – VALKENSWEG

Hangar

A'DAM Toren

21 HANGAR

Hangar is one of the newest restaurants on the banks of the IJ in Amsterdam North. A semi-cylindrical, corrugated metal hangar in green and white has been transformed into a trendy restaurant that's open from lunch to dinnertime. It's got a warm interior with a beautiful marble bar, and a seasonal menu.

AAMBEELDSTRAAT 36, HANGAR.AMSTERDAM, 020-3638657, BUS: 38 & 105 – HAMERSTRAAT

12 THE ROLLING ROCK KITCHEN

It's all about photography and music at Rolling Rock Kitchen, aka Rock. Not live rock, mind you, despite the guitars hanging from the ceiling of this bar, but the atmosphere is rock 'n' roll, and the food is simple but good.

DISTELWEG 113, ROLLINGROCKKITCHEN.COM, BUS: 38 – DISTELWEG

31 MOON

Moon is on the nineteenth floor of the A'DAM Toren. This restaurant rotates through its circle once every hour, giving you a unique dining experience with an awesome 360° view of the city. A different artist plays guest chef every other month at this fine restaurant.

OVERHOEKSPLEIN 1, ADAMTOREN.NL, FERRY TO BUIKSLOTERWEG

14 CAFÉ DE CEUVEL

Café De Ceuvel is *the* hipster hotspot in North. Everything revolves around sustainability, from the recycled materials from which the eatery was built to the food, delicious farm-to-table dishes made with ingredients from local suppliers.

KORTE PAPAVERWEG 4, CAFEDECEUVEL.NL, 020-2296210, BUS: 34, 35, 391, 394 & 763 – MOSPLEIN

Café De Ceuvel

28 THE COFFEE VIRUS

The name gives it away, but in all honesty this is no ordinary coffee bar. The coffee served here is made from beans from Amsterdam roasteries, served to you in a refurbished Shell laboratory canteen in which creative minds can also rent workspace. They serve sandwiches, salads and toasties at lunchtime.

OVERHOEKSPLEIN 2, THECOFFEEVIRUS.NL, FERRY TO BUIKSLOTERWEG

TIP!
If you go to Amsterdam North, don't omit a visit to A'DAM Toren from your to-do list.

30 MADAM

Madam is A'DAM Toren's panoramic restaurant, located on the twentieth floor. By day, Madam is part of the LOOKOUT experien-ce, but once the sun goes down it transforms into the highest nightclub in Amsterdam. Then you can revel in its extensive, international à la carte menu and its stunning view.

OVERHOEKSPLEIN 1, ADAMTOREN.NL, FERRY TO BUIKSLOTERWEG

27 THT

THT is the Tolhuistuin's restaurant: a cultural meeting spot with events. Tolhuistuin renovated a former Shell canteen, turning it into somewhere to have lunch and dinner every day, and its menu is packed with dishes with an international twist. The terrace is a must when the weather's good.

IJPROMENADE 2, THT.NL, 020-7604820, FERRY TO BUIKSLOTERWEG

24 OEDIPUS TAPROOM

The Amsterdam microbrewery Oedipus has its own taproom in North! A paradise for beer fans, as they have no less than twelve different kinds of craft beer on tap. Take your seat at one of the long beer tables from Friday to Sunday.

GEDEMPT HAMERKANAAL 85, OEDIPUSBREWING.COM, BUS: 38 & 105 – HAVIKSLAAN

The Coffee Virus

Hotel De Goudfazant

22 HOTEL DE GOUDFAZANT

Hotel De Goudfazant occupies a former car garage and retains its authentic industrial look. It was one of the first restaurants to transform an old building into a hotspot. It's not a hotel, despite what the name suggests, but it *is* an extraordinary restaurant that's packed every night of the week because of the quality of the food and the well-priced menu.

AAMBEELDSTRAAT 10, HOTELDEGOUDFAZANT.NL, 020-6365170, BUS: 38 & 105 – HAVIKSLAAN

2 LOETJE AAN HET IJ

The renowned steak restaurant Loetje is *also* on the IJ! Bonus feature: there are jetties for you to moor your boat. In other words, a good destination when you start to feel peckish after a day on the water. The Bali steak is legendary and a must-try.

WERFKADE 14, LOETJEAANTIJ.LOETJE.COM, 020-2088000, FERRY TO NDSM WHARF

3 PONTSTATION

This is an organic snack bar close to the point where the ferry to NDSM Wharf drops you off. You can get the most delicious organic fries, hot dogs and other snacks for lunch or a quick bite in the evening, which can be nice after a day at Pllek's city beach. A fries bar of a different order!

MS. VAN RIEMSDIJKWEG 28, PONTSTATION.NL, 020-6330224, FERRY TO NDSM WHARF

Smaaqt

16 SMAAQT

A brasserie that is all a brasserie should be: warm and atmospheric. Smaaqt's interior has a rugged cool look, and you'll find this place on the Van der Pekstraat, where the Pek Market is held a few days every week. All the ingredients used in Smaaqt's kitchen come straight from the market.

VAN DER PEKSTRAAT 79, SMAAQT.NL, 020-6369063, BUS: 38 – MEIDOORNPLEIN

15 DE SOEPBOER

If you fancy some soup, go to the Soepboer! They make seasonal soups, served to you with home-baked bread. There's a small terrace in summer, or you can snuggle up next to the window to watch the activity on the Pekmarkt.

VAN DER PEKSTRAAT 93, DESOEPBOER.NL, 020-3541564, BUS: 38 – GENTIAANSTRAAT

19 FASHION & TEA

Fashion & Tea is on the increasingly hip Van der Pekstraat. In addition to a nice cup of tea and thickly layered sandwiches, you can have a good browse. This hotspot sells jewellery, watches, leather goods and clothing for men and women from well-known and less-well-known labels.

VAN DER PEKSTRAAT 40, FASHIONANDTEA.NL, 020-7530450, BUS: 38 & 105 – MEIDOORNPLEIN

SHOPPING

10 NEEF LOUIS

If you're in an industrial neighbourhood, you want to be able to shop for industrial stuff, too. Neef Louis sells fantastic vintage and designer furniture. You can come back every week to feast your eyes, and there's nothing you can think of that they don't sell. New stuff arrives every week.

PAPAVERWEG 46, NEEFLOUIS.NL, 020-4869354, BUS: 38 – KLAPROZENWEG/ RIDDERSPOORWEG

TIP!
The up-and-coming Van der Pekstraat is where to shop in North.

11 VAN DIJK & KO

The vintage store Van Dijk & Ko is next to Neef Louis. Where at Neef Louis you're surrounded by lots of industrial stuff, here the items are mostly used and vintage with a rural touch. Even if you don't plan to buy anything, you can nose around and find inspiration here!

PAPAVERWEG 47, VANDIJKENKO.NL, 020-6841524, BUS: 38 – KLAPROZENWEG/ RIDDERSPOORWEG

NORTH

17 PEK MARKET

There's an archetypal Dutch market on the North Meidoornplein. This is where the Pek Market (Pekmarkt) opens every Wednesday, Friday and Saturday, each day a different theme: Friday the organic and farmers market, Saturday the mixed market. Besides food, there are also stalls selling vintage items and other curiosities.

HEIMANSWEG, PEKMARKT.NL, BUS: 38 & 105 – MEIDOORNPLEIN

13 BLOM & BLOM

Blom & Blom is where to go if you're looking for something butch and unique for the home. Two brothers scour abandoned factories in East Germany for the nicest looking industrial lamps

Blom & Blom

Pek & Kleren

Woodies at Berlin

and furniture, which they restore and sell in their shop. Fun detail: each piece has its own passport with more information on its origin.

CHRYSANTENSTRAAT 20, BLOMANDBLOM.COM, BUS: 38 – CHRYSANTENSTRAAT

18 PEK & KLEREN

Mini department store or concept store? Hard to say, but what's certain is that at Pek & Kleren (meaning clothes) on the Van der Pekstraat you can have a cup of coffee, and there's something for every budget in their constantly changing collection of women's and men's clothing, shoes, jewellery, home accessories and other gadgets.

VAN DER PEKSTRAAT 56-58, PEK-EN-KLEREN.NL, BUS: 38 & 105 – MEIDOORNPLEIN

6 WOODIES AT BERLIN

Woodies at Berlin on the NDSM Wharf sells a combination of vintage designer furniture, lighting and proprietary products – there's a workshop at the back of the store where they design and make furniture themselves. Nice to have something made to your style.

MS. VAN RIEMSDIJKWEG 51, WOODIESATBERLIN.NL, FERRY TO NDSM WHARF

8 IJ-HALLEN

The largest flea market in Europe is in Amsterdam. Once a month two massive industrial halls on the NDSM Wharf are transformed into markets where you can buy all kinds of second-hand items, from junk to gems. It is always packed.

TT. NEVERITAWEG 15, IJHALLEN.NL, 0229-581598, FERRY TO NDSM WHARF

MY LITTLE BLACK BOOK

NOTES

INDEX IN ALFABETICAL ORDER

INDEX

THEMATIC INDEX

INDEX

PSSSSSST...

Enjoyed checking out all the tips in *The Amsterdam City Guide* and love to travel? Then you must get yourself a copy of *Wanderlust* and download the Your Little Black Book app!

WANDERLUST

Wanderlust combines travel, style and food, along with my personal travel tips and tricks for making the most of all your trips.
AVAILABLE IN DUTCH AT BOOKSHOPS AND BOL.COM

YLBB - APP

You'll find all the Amsterdam spots featured on Yourlittleblackbook.me at your fingertips via the handy smartphone app. Search your app store for *Amsterdam City Guide* – yourlbb and discover the city through my eyes!
AVAILABLE FOR ANDROID AND IOS USERS